Economics, Law, and Institutions in Asia Pacific

Series Editor
Makoto Yano, Research Institute of Economy, Trade and Industry (RIETI), Tokyo, Japan

The Asia Pacific region is expected to steadily enhance its economic and political presence in the world during the twenty-first century. At the same time, many serious economic and political issues remain unresolved in the region. To further academic enquiry and enhance readers' understanding about this vibrant region, the present series, Economics, Law, and Institutions in Asia Pacific, aims to present cutting-edge research on the Asia Pacific region and its relationship with the rest of the world. For countries in this region to achieve robust economic growth, it is of foremost importance that they improve the quality of their markets, as history shows that healthy economic growth cannot be achieved without high-quality markets. High-quality markets can be established and maintained only under a well-designed set of rules and laws, without which competition will not flourish. Based on these principles, this series places a special focus on economic, business, legal, and institutional issues geared towards the healthy development of Asia Pacific markets. The series considers book proposals for scientific research, either theoretical or empirical, that is related to the theme of improving market quality and has policy implications for the Asia Pacific region. The types of books that will be considered for publication include research monographs as well as relevant proceedings. The series show-cases work by Asia-Pacific based researchers but also encourages the work of social scientists not limited to the Asia Pacific region. Each proposal and final manuscript is subject to evaluation by the editorial board and experts in the field.

More information about this series at http://www.springer.com/series/13451

Akiko Kamesaka · Franz Waldenberger
Editors

Governance, Risk and Financial Impact of Mega Disasters

Lessons from Japan

Springer

Editors
Akiko Kamesaka
School of Business Administration
Financial Markets Research Center
Aoyama Gakuin University
Tokyo, Japan

Franz Waldenberger
German Institute for Japanese Studies
Tokyo, Japan

Munich School of Management
Ludwig-Maximilians-Universität München
Munich, Germany

ISSN 2199-8620 ISSN 2199-8639 (electronic)
Economics, Law, and Institutions in Asia Pacific
ISBN 978-981-13-9004-3 ISBN 978-981-13-9005-0 (eBook)
https://doi.org/10.1007/978-981-13-9005-0

This Springer imprint is published by the registered company Springer Nature Singapore Pte Ltd.
The registered company address is: 152 Beach Road, #21-01/04 Gateway East, Singapore 189721, Singapore

Preface

This book is the outcome of a research project analyzing the impact of a major earthquake on the fiscal conditions of the Japanese government. The project was conducted in 2016 by a team comprising four of the authors of this book, including the two editors: Akiko Kamesaka, Soichiro Moridaira, Motohiro Sato, and Franz Waldenberger. The research was supported by Munich Re Japan, which provided the funding for a research assistant.

The research findings were presented and discussed at the workshop "Governance and Financial Aspects of Catastrophic/Systemic Risks" jointly organized by the German Institute for Japanese Studies and Aoyama Gakuin University Research Institute in Tokyo in September 2016. Takahiro Tsuda and Ortwin Renn joined the research group for the workshop. Tsuda's overview on Japan's disaster risk financing schemes and Renn's paper on the governance of systemic risk are included as Chaps. 2 and 6 in this book. In addition, Julius Weitzdörfer and Simon Beard agreed to contribute a study on the "double loan" problems resulting from damage to privately owned buildings. It appears as Chap. 4.

The publication was supported by the German Institute for Japanese Studies under its research program "Risks and Opportunities in Japan—Challenges in the Face of an Increasingly Uncertain Future," Aoyama Gakuin University Research Institute under its research topic "Comparative Studies on Stock Markets," and JSPS KAKENHI Grant Number JP16H03640.

Tokyo, Japan

Akiko Kamesaka
Franz Waldenberger

Contents

Editors and Contributors

About the Editors

Akiko Kamesaka is Professor at Aoyama Gakuin University in Tokyo Japan, School of Business Administration. She is also the Director of the Financial Markets Research Center, Aoyama Gakuin University, and she was a visiting research fellow at the Economic and Social Research Institute, Cabinet Office, Government of Japan. She has worked as an accountant at a large accounting firm in Tokyo, and has studied at the University of Tokyo graduate school of economics. Her interests include analysis on well-being, worldview, and investor behavior, and she has many publications in economics and finance. She received the Ibbotson Associates Japan Research Award at the Asia-Pacific Finance Association/ Pacific-Basin Financial Management Society/Financial Management Association joint conference for her research on investor behavior in Japan. She was invited to speak at a panel on subjective well-being and sustainability at the 4th OECD World Forum, and has presented her work at many other large conferences and meetings. She has been conducting investor surveys in Japan with Prof. Robert J. Shiller, who was awarded the Nobel Prize in Economic Sciences in 2013.

Franz Waldenberger obtained his Ph.D. in economics from the University of Cologne. After positions with the German Monopolies Commission and the German Institute of Japanese Studies (DIJ), he became Professor for Japanese Economy at Munich University. He has been visiting professor at various Japanese universities, including the University of Tokyo, Tsukuba University, Hitotsubashi University, and Osaka City University. He serves as Editor in Chief of Contemporary Japan and as member of the editorial board of *Asian Business & Management*. Presently, he is on leave from Munich University to head the DIJ in Tokyo. His research focuses on the Japanese economy and corporate governance. Professor Waldenberger is member of the German Japan Forum and member of the board of the Japanese-German Business Association (DJW).

Contributors

Simon Beard is a Senior Research Associate and Academic Program Director at the Centre for the Study of Existential Risk, University of Cambridge and an Affiliated Researcher at the Institute for Futures Studies. He has a background in moral and political philosophy with a focus on distributive justice and population ethics. He also has a background in political advocacy having twice stood for election to the Parliament of the United Kingdom and serves as an advisor to the All-Party Parliamentary Group for Future Generations.

Soichiro Moridaira is Emeritus Professor of Keio University. He was a Professor of Finance at the Graduate School of Finance, Waseda University, a Professor of Finance at the Faculty of Policy Management at Keio University and an Associate Professor of Finance at Fukushima University. He earned his Ph.D. in finance and insurance areas from McCombs School of Business, the University of Texas at Austin. His research can be classified into three major areas: (1) asset pricing and its application to real and financial problems, (2) risk management, especially credit risk and natural disaster modeling, (3) computational finance. He participated in Catastrophic Natural Disasters Risk Finance Study of Cabinet Office, Government of Japan, which is closely related to the topic of this publication.

Ortwin Renn is Scientific Director at the International Institute for Advanced Sustainability Studies (IASS) in Potsdam (Germany) since February 1, 2016. He continues to serve as acting chair of the Stuttgart Research Center for Interdisciplinary Risk and Innovation Studies at the University of Stuttgart (ZIRIUS) and as Scientific Director of the nonprofit company DIALOGIK, a research institute for the investigation of communication and participation processes. Renn is Adjunct Professor for "Integrated Risk Analysis" at Stavanger University (Norway) and Affiliate Professor for "Risk Governance" at Beijing Normal University. Ortwin Renn has a doctoral degree in social psychology from the University of Cologne. His career included teaching and research positions at Clark University (Worcester, USA), the Swiss Institute of Technology (Zuerich), and the Center of Technology Assessment (Stuttgart). His honors include the National Cross of Merit Order, an honorary doctorate from the Swiss Institute of Technology, an honorary professorship at the Technical University Munich and the "Distinguished Achievement Award" of the Society for Risk Analysis (SRA).

Motohiro Sato is Professor at the Graduate school of Economics and School of International and Public Policy Hitotsubashi University. He obtained his Ph.D. in Economics at Queen's University, Canada. His field of research includes fiscal federalism, tax, and public finance. He served as chair of the Project Team on the Earthquake Insurance at the Ministry of Finance. He has been member of the government tax commission and several government committees. He is now Co-Editor of Japanese Economic Review and Associate Editor of the Journal of

Public Economics. He served as a board member of the Japan Institute of Public Finance. He received the Mainichi Economist Award in 2012 for his book on local tax reform and the Ishikawa Award from the Japanese Economic Association.

Takahiro Tsuda is a Director, Office of Planning and Coordination for International Affairs, International Bureau, Ministry of Finance. Prior to the current position, he was responsible for various international finance issues in the Ministry, including G7/G20 coordination, APEC, IMF, and bilateral cooperation with China, India, and South Korea. He also worked for the Budget Bureau during 2016–18, and covered macro-fiscal research and budget for agriculture, fishery, and forestry. He also worked for IMF as a financial sector expert during 2010–13. His area of interest includes sovereign debt issues, local currency bond markets, and fiscal policy. He is a CFA charter holder.

Julius Weitzdörfer is Director of Studies in Law at Darwin College Cambridge and an Affiliated Lecturer at the Faculty of Law, University of Cambridge. With a background in Japanese studies and in nuclear-, disaster-, and financial law, he is a postdoctoral Research Associate at the Centre for the Study of Existential Risk (CSER), where he works on the project “Managing Extreme Technological Risk”. His expertise lies in the law and governance of extreme risk, especially with regard to unprecedented incidents, crises, and disasters. Working in three languages and across four jurisdictions, he adopts comparative, policy-focussed, socio-legal, and economic approaches.

Chapter 1
Financial Impact of Mega Disasters

Franz Waldenberger and Akiko Kamesaka

1 Introduction

1.1 Background

International statistics indicate that total inflation adjusted losses caused by catastrophic natural disasters more than tripled between the 1980s and the present decade (Table 1). The number of catastrophic disasters reveals no clear trend over the same period, which means that events caused increasingly higher losses. This partly reflects an increase in the devastating power of events, but it can also be attributed to economic growth and urbanization. The first trend implies a higher productive value, the latter a higher regional concentration of assets. Both implications lead to higher values at risk.

As a country regularly exposed to earthquakes and tropical cyclones (typhoons) Japan features prominently in natural disaster reports. Three of the five costliest earthquakes during the last 30 years occurred in Japan (Munich Re 2019). Between 1990 and 2017, four earthquakes in Japan were classified as catastrophic based on the number of fatalities and damages (Table 2a). The number corresponds to 4.4% of the respective worldwide number. Japan covers only about 0.3% of the combined land area of all countries of the world. This means that its exposure to catastrophic earthquakes was almost 15-times higher than the world average.

Japan's share in worldwide losses caused by catastrophic earthquakes between 1990 and 2017 was 40 (!) per cent, almost ten times more than its share in the number of events. This reflects the strong power of the earthquakes hitting Japan,

F. Waldenberger (✉)
German Institute for Japanese Studies, Tokyo, Japan
e-mail: waldenberger@dijtokyo.org

A. Kamesaka
Aoyama Gakuin University, Tokyo, Japan

A. Kamesaka and F. Waldenberger (eds.), *Governance, Risk and Financial Impact of Mega Disasters*, Economics, Law, and Institutions in Asia Pacific,
https://doi.org/10.1007/978-981-13-9005-0_1

Table 1 Occurrence and impact of catastrophic disasters over time

	Number	Fatalities	Losses (Bn USD)	Insured (Bn USD)	Insurance coverage (%)
1980–1989	185	152,940	366	40	11
1990–1999	318	336,700	887	159	18
2000–2009	219	701,196	977	241	25
2010–2017	215	291,685	1,126	329	29

Source Munich Re, NatCatService, https://natcatservice.munichre.com. *Notes* Disasters are classified as catastrophic if they cause more than 1,000 fatalities or losses of more than 3 bn USD in high income countries, for countries with lower income lower thresholds apply; losses are inflation adjusted. Japan share is calculated on the basis of the world total including Japan

Table 2 Occurrence and impact of catastrophic disasters—Japan and the rest of the world

	Number	Fatalities	Losses (Bn USD)	Insured (Bn USD)	Insurance coverage (%)
(a) Catastrophic earthquakes 1990–2017					
Japan	4	22,561	303	40	13
Rest of the world	87	721,780	467	73	16
Japan's share (%)	4.4	3.0	39.4	35.4	
(b) Catastrophic tropical cyclones 1990–2017					
Japan	6	199	42	73	45
Rest of the world	185	358,368	1,002	370	37
Japan's share (%)	3.1	0.1	4.0	19.7	

Source Munich Re, NatCatService. https://natcatservice.munichre.com. *Notes* Disasters are classified as catastrophic if they cause more than 1,000 fatalities or losses of more than 3 bn USD in high income countries, for countries with lower income lower thresholds apply; losses are inflation adjusted. Japan's share is calculated on the basis of the world total including Japan

but it is also related to the size and development of Japan's economy. As the second largest high-income economy in the world, earthquakes are bound to inflict high damages on productive assets. In addition, economic activity in Japan is highly concentrated. The agglomeration belt spanning from the Kanto region around Tokyo to the Kansai region around Osaka, Kyoto and Kobe generate 54% of the country's taxable income, but cover only 14% of its land area (World Bank 2019). Among the four mega-earthquakes, the Hanshin-Awaji earthquake of 1995 hit the densely populated Kansai region.

Japan's share in the number of catastrophic tropical cyclones between 1990 and 2017 was 3.1% (Table 2b). Its share in related losses amounted to four per cent, which contrasts sharply with the earthquake statistics. The fact that the typhoons that hit Japan were by international comparison less devastating than earthquakes is mainly due to their weaker power and to the strong resilience of Japan's urban infrastructure. Major damages, such as landslides, occurred in rural areas, where infrastructures tend to be more vulnerable to storms and heavy rainfall.

It is interesting to note, that insurance coverage of natural disasters has worldwide been well below 50%. In Japan, 45% of losses from tropical cyclones had been insured compared to an average of 37% for all other countries (Table 2b). The coverage drops to below 20% in the case of losses from catastrophic earthquakes. Here the ratio for Japan is only 13%, which is even lower than the average of 16% for other countries. It seems that either the willingness or the ability to insure against earthquake risks is lower than in the case meteorological risks like typhoons. The issue will be taken up in the next section.

This book is the outcome of a research project on fiscal resilience conducted in 2016 by four of the authors with two additional contributions solicited from international researchers in the field. Findings were presented at the workshop "Governance and Financial Aspects of Catastrophic/Systemic Risks" jointly organized by the German Institute for Japanese Studies and Aoyama Gakuin University Research Institute in Tokyo in September 2016.

Four of the five articles collected in this book focus on the actual or expected financial and economic impact of mega disasters in Japan with three of them taking as example the Great East Japan Earthquake of 11 March 2011 as well as the ensuing tsunami and nuclear catastrophe in Fukushima. Although explicit comparisons with other countries are not drawn, the findings should be instructive for other countries given that Japan is most exposed to such risks and has suffered the highest losses (Table 1). There is therefore a lot to learn from how the Japanese government, private investors and households deal with and are impacted by the risks of mega earthquakes. The fifth and last article approaches the topic from a conceptual perspective by applying the framework of systemic risk.

Before summarizing the content of the articles, the next two section will discuss two common underlying themes. The first theme relates to the question of insurance as a precautionary measure to the financial risks associated with earthquakes. The second theme concerns investor behavior after mega disasters, such as the Great East Japan Earthquake.

1.2 Insuring Against Earthquake Risk

Seen by the coverage of losses, earthquake risk is much less insured against than for example meteorological risk (Table 2). This is especially true for Japan. It is surprising for two reasons. Given the country's extreme exposure to earthquake risk one would expect that comprehensive insurance schemes are in place. Precautionary measures might even be prescribed by law or demanded by financial investors who ultimately have to bear the risk if borrowers become insolvent as a result of an earthquake.

The particularly low level of insurance in Japan is also surprising, because the Japanese people are generally considered to have a very low level of risk tolerance (Hofstede et al. 2010). In fact, households and corporations exhibit behavior that reflects a high degree of risk aversion. Japanese households tend to invest 80% of their financial wealth in so-called safe assets like cash, bank accounts or life insurance products (Bank of Japan 2018). Japanese companies are also considered to be more risk averse than their international counterparts as seen by lower levels of return on equity and large cash holdings (OECD 2015).

So why do households and corporations shy away from insurance against earthquake risk? It is not because insurance schemes do not exist. As Takahiro Tsuda shows in Chap. 2, Japan introduced a public earthquake insurance scheme for households in 1966. It is offered as an option attached to fire insurance contracts and reinsured by the government to limit the burden for private insurers. Although the market penetration rate has been rising since the Hanshin-Awaji Earthquake in 1995, it is still below 30% (Tsuda, Chap. 2, Fig. 4). Lack of insurance surfaces as a socioeconomic issue in the aftermath of disasters, when households confront so called "double loan" problems (Weitzdörfer and Beard, Chap. 4).

In 2012, Waldenberger (2013) conducted a survey among 107 industry experts asking for their assessment of the following six possible hypotheses as to why demand for household earthquake insurance might be sub-optimal: (1) earthquake risks are too difficult to insure, (2) households underestimate the risks, (3) they lack information or (4) they free ride in expectation of public support after a larger quake, (5) the product is not sufficiently promoted or (6) it is not attractive due to regulatory constraints. The answers to most suggested explanations varied and were in the aggregate indecisive. Agreement among respondents could only be established with regard to the hypothesis that households lack information (hypothesis 3). The lack of information might be related to insufficient marketing efforts (hypothesis 5) on the side of insurance companies as they only distribute the government product without earning extra profit on it.

The situation is even worse in the case of small and medium sized enterprises (SME). A survey conducted in 2016 among SME in regions hit by major earthquakes showed that only nine per cent had their business insured against earthquake and only 21% had household insurance (Sompo Risk Management 2017). The ratio for business insurance went up to 15% after the quake, indicating a positive reevaluation of the benefits of being insured.

The government applies a wide range of support measures for business in response to large disasters (Sompo Risk Management 2017, Tsuda Chap. 2), which means that companies can potentially draw from three different funds to cover losses from disasters. They might use internal reserves, payments from insurance, if they hold respective policies, or as a third option, they can count on post-disaster public support. The importance of government support is not only evidenced by the existence of extensive post-disaster relief measures. It also shows up in regional bankruptcy statistics. In the Tohoku region, which was hit by the Great East Japan Earthquake on 11 March 2011, the number of bankruptcies declined relative to the national trend in the years following the disaster (Fig. 1). There is a simple explanation to this

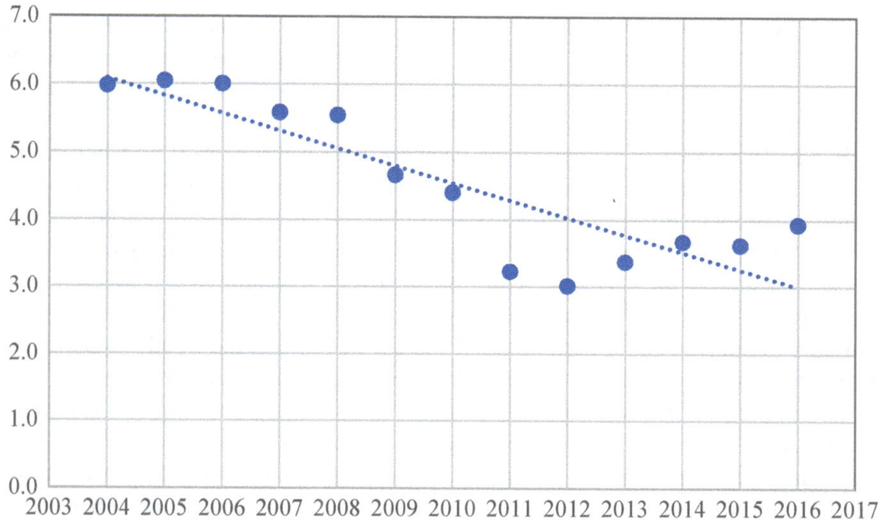

Fig. 1 Ratio of number of bankruptcies in the Tohoku region to the number of nation-wide bankruptcies in per cent. *Source* Teikoku Databank, own calculations

counter-intuitive observation. Post-disaster support measures have to be provided quickly. They are hardly able to discriminate between originally healthy and failing firms. This means that firms, which would have gone out of business even without the disaster, receive support that enables them to survive. As a result, the bankruptcy rate will be lower directly after the disaster.

The Japanese government, which emphasizes that corporations, especially SMEs, should buy more insurance as part of their business continuity planning (Cabinet Office 2017), obviously faces a dilemma. For private companies, public post-disaster business support programs represent a substitute for disaster insurance. In order to increase earthquake insurance, the government would either have to convincingly restrict post-disaster support measures, to make them dependent on whether companies have insurance coverage, or otherwise create strong tax-incentives for insurance or even make earthquake insurance per se compulsory. While the Japanese government cannot be expected to commit to the first option, it may well consider one or a combination of the other three options.

1.3 Investor Behavior

How do investors react to mega disasters like large earthquakes? Earthquakes represent shocks that are difficult to anticipate. The reaction therefore happens after the event. In Chap. 5, Soichiro Moridaira looks at how the stock market reevaluated the risk of investing in insurance and electricity companies after the Great East Japan

Earthquake and the ensuing nuclear disaster. This introductory section provides a more general background on stock and foreign exchange market reactions to the disaster from 11 March 2011 by also differentiating between domestic and foreign investors. It is based on Kamesaka (2013).

Figure 2 shows the movement of the Japanese stock price index TOPIX before and after the Great East Japan Earthquake. The index had been rising before the earthquake, but dropped afterwards. Since March 11 was a Friday, the reaction occurred at the beginning of the following week. However, recovery started already in the same week. Considering the very large shock, the recovery was quite fast. It was followed by a period of stability. The further decline late July/early August 2011 was probably caused by concerns about the impact of the US deficit and the floods in Bangkok, where many subsidiaries of Japanese manufacturing companies were located.

The pattern of the stock market reaction to the Great East Japan Earthquake is consistent with the analysis presented by Motohiro Sato in Chap. 3. There is first a large downturn of the economy followed by an upswing due to expected reconstruction works. Overall, the market responded very quickly and strongly to the shock.

Figure 3 shows the Japanese yen to US dollar exchange rate. When negative events occur in Japan, the Japanese yen tends to appreciate. Right after the March 11 earthquake, the yen spiked very high. The pattern can partly be explained by the expectation, that a negative event will create strong demands of funding to cover losses and to achieve a smooth recovery. A large portion of these funds will have to be provided from abroad causing an increase in demand for yen. A higher yen improves Japan's terms of trade, i.e. it makes the purchases of foreign goods and

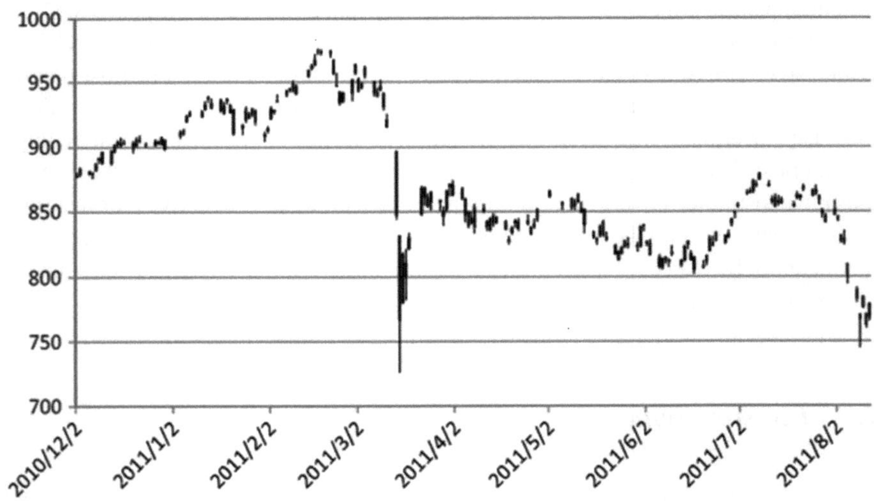

Fig. 2 Tokyo Stock Price Index (TOPIX) before and after the Great East Japan Earthquake. *Source* Kamesaka (2013)

Fig. 3 The yen-dollar exchange rate. *Source* Kamesaka (2013)

services cheaper. This is especially beneficial, when imports are needed to cover supply shortages following a mega disaster.

A closer look at the behavior of foreign investors in the Japanese stock market reveals, that their additional purchases of Japanese stocks directly after the earthquake also contributed to the sharp rise in the value of the yen against the dollar. Net purchases by foreign investors sharply increased right after the earthquake (Fig. 4). Japanese securities firms and financial institutions were on the seller side.

The behavior of foreign investors was striking because it was different from their typical trading behavior in the Japanese stock market (Hood et al. 2013). They usually behave like "momentum traders" who try to benefit from a trend. They should therefore have been net sellers when the market declined. Instead they behaved like "contrarian traders" that buy and sell against the trend. Being net buyers during the downward movement, foreign investors helped to reduce volatility and stabilize the market.

1.4 Outline of the Book

Chapter 2 introduces the Japanese government's disaster risk finance (DRF) framework. According to the author, Takahiro Tsuda, it is the first attempt to present Japan's DRF schemes and policies in a comprehensive and systematic manner. The chapter provides an overview of the framework as well as a detailed description of its various parts, with a special focus on the public earthquake insurance scheme and

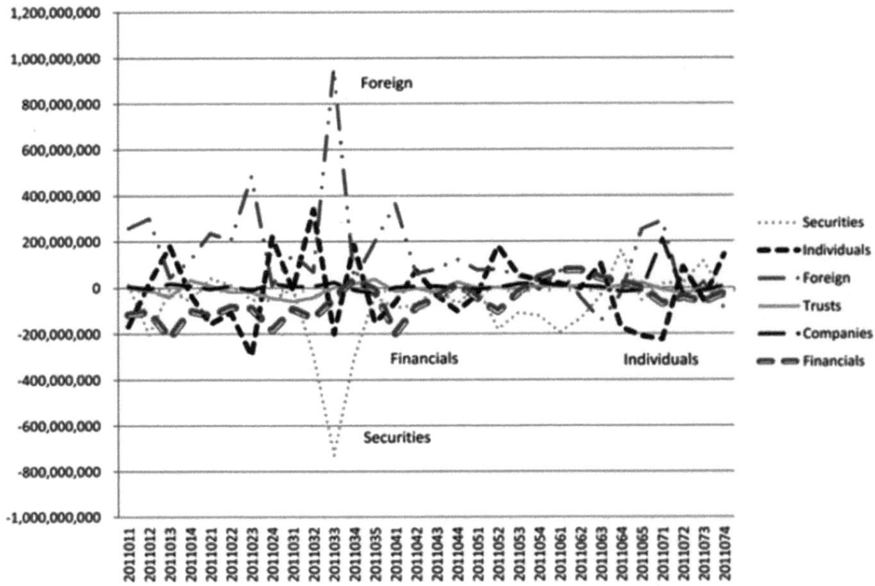

Fig. 4 Weekly net purchases of main investor groups. *Source* Kamesaka (2013)

fiscal frameworks for recovery and reconstruction. Their implementation is exemplified with reference to recent disasters. Finally, Japan's various efforts to promote DRF internationally are outlined and explained. Overall, the chapter demonstrates that given the country's long and severe exposure to natural disasters, especially earthquakes, the government has a complete set of DRF measures in place. Japan is willing to take a leading role in the international arena by leveraging its experience through bilateral and multilateral agreements. Besides these achievements, Tsuda also points out potentials for improvement. These relate to the further penetration of earthquake insurance and the fine-tuning of public reconstruction funds.

The Japanese government carries the highest debt burden among OECD countries. For the time being the situation seems safe, as Japan's private domestic sector is generating enough savings to finance the funding needs of the government. However, it can be expected that domestic funds will eventually run out. In this case the Japanese government will have to rely on foreign investors. This will lead to higher financing costs increasing the probability of default. How does such a setting affect the Japanese government's ability to implement its DRF scheme in the case of a mega earthquake hitting Tokyo? How will another mega disaster affect the fiscal stability of the Japanese government?

In Chap. 3, Motohiro Sato analyses the second question. Within the framework of a simple Keynesian macroeconomic model, he analyzes the impact of a mega-earthquake hitting Tokyo in 2020. Besides the no-earthquake and no-fiscal-consolidation reference case, the analysis accounts for five contextual scenarios depending on whether and when the government undertakes fiscal consolidation and whether the economy is booming or in a recession. Outcomes for the different scenarios are estimated by applying the Monte-Carlo Simulation method. The results show that whereas under all earthquake scenarios economic growth will soon be restored due to reconstruction demand, interest rates on government bonds are likely to increase faster in comparison to the reference case except when fiscal consolidation is undertaken. Based on the model and the simulation results, Sato concludes that even without the occurrence of a mega earthquake, the Japanese government will inevitably confront a fiscal crisis. The mega-disaster will only function as a catalyst, causing the fiscal crisis to happen earlier.

Chapter 4 complements Chaps. 2 and 3 by looking at the financial burdens on the private sector. Julius Weitzdörfer and Simon Beard examine problems of disaster-induced financial distress from a legal, economic and social justice perspective. They do this both qualitatively and quantitatively, focusing on residential loans and using the victims of the 11 March 2011 tsunami as their sample. Applying doctrinal and systematic analysis, the authors set out the broad array of law and policy solutions launched by the government to tackle disaster-induced private debt. On this basis, they first assess the strengths and weaknesses of these measures in terms of their practical adequacy to prevent and mitigate financial hardship and then examine them against multiple dimensions of justice. A central issue are so-called "double loan" issues facing households and small business who suffered high uninsured damage on their property, mainly houses, while still having to pay back loans taken up to finance the now damaged property. Whereas the government offers financial support to business, households cannot expect such relief. Weitzdörfer and Beard offer suggestions for improving financial disaster recovery by taking a prospective approach, thus preventing the snowballing of disaster-related losses. A key point in their proposal are measures to further promote the demand for earthquake insurance.

In highly advanced economies like Japan disaster risks are partly borne by investors and allocated across financial markets. Section 1.3 above already provided some general background information about how the stock and foreign exchange markets reacted to the Great East Japan Earthquake. In Chap. 5, Soichiro Moridaira presents a detailed analysis on how the disaster affected the risk assessment of stocks reflected in the share prices of electricity and insurance companies. The starting point of his analysis is the observation that in comparison to the strong downturn caused by the global financial crisis of 2007–2008 the 11 March 2011 disaster had a much lower impact on the NIKKEI 225 index. However, the picture completely changes when looking at the credit or default risk imputed in share prices. Applying this perspective, the 11 March 2011 event had an even stronger, though less prolonged impact than the world financial crisis, especially for relatively smaller companies, which are not included in the NIKKEI 225 index. The analysis of Japan's ten regional electric power companies shows that for the nine companies operating nuclear power plants the Fukushima nuclear disaster not only increased the risk assessment for listed stock of TEPCO, the owner of the plant, but similarly for all other eight companies. Moridaira concludes, that the disaster turned the operation of nuclear power plants into a business that is damaging corporate value. Performing the same analysis for the stock of non-life insurance companies reveals no particular changes. Moridaira contributes this to their preparedness for the disaster and to the role of the government as re-insurer for the earthquake insurance for households.

The economic impact of mega-disasters like catastrophic earthquakes is not limited to damages of houses, offices, factories and infrastructures. There are in addition income losses due to the interruption of production. In a global production system, such income losses tend to be nationally and internationally dispersed. In the case of the Great East Japan Earthquake, most income losses due to short-term production downtimes were caused by disruptions of trans-regional supply chains either because of damages incurred by vital suppliers or because of the interruption of transportation infrastructures (Waldenberger and Eilker 2012). Again, as the March 11 earthquake shows, the risks associated with of a mega earthquake are not necessarily the trembles alone. The Great East Japan Earthquake induced consequent disasters like the tsunami and the destruction of nuclear power plants in Fukushima. In his memoirs of the crisis surrounding the nuclear disaster, Naoto Kan, at the time prime minister of Japan and in this function also head of the national crisis team, recounts two critical situations where only lucky coincidences prevented the outbreak of a nuclear catastrophe that would have necessitated mass evacuation including Tokyo (Kan 2017). Last, but not least, the analysis in Chap. 2 suggests, that a future mega earthquake in Japan will likely result in a severe fiscal crisis given the high indebtedness of the Japanese government.

Through their impact on national and international supply chains and by causing a chain of subsequent crises, mega earthquakes bear characteristics of systemic risk. In the final chapter of this book, Ortwin Renn, presents a framework for the analysis of systemic risk by describing its major characteristics and by outlining governance approaches for improving resilience. Systemic risks can be classified according to the degree of complexity, uncertainty and ambiguity involved in their analysis. Whereas complexity may be resolved by applying adequate probabilistic risk modelling, uncertainty requires the integrative evaluation of different stakeholder perspectives. In addition, in the case of ambiguity, discourses need to include the wider public not only for the sake of raising awareness, but also in order to reach consensus about normative questions, which expert knowledge alone cannot adequately answer.

1.5 Concluding Remarks

The chapters in this book introduce new scholarly work on the financial and economic impact of mega-disasters by taking Japan's experiences as an example. They also make research by Japanese scholars originally published in Japanese available to a broader audience. Last, but not least, taken together the chapters offer a systematic overview of public disaster financing schemes with a broad analysis of actual as well as possible impacts on the financial positions of the government and private households. This is complemented by research findings on the reaction of capital markets to the Great East Japan earthquake and the ensuing nuclear disaster. The final chapter on the governance of systemic risk allows the reader to put the preceding analysis into a yet broader risk management context.

In combination, the findings offer important lessons. First, the Japanese case is instructive not only by showing how mega disasters impact an advanced economy, but also by teaching us what governments can do to allocate the financial risk inherent in natural disasters, and what they could do even better. Second, whereas the Great East Japan Earthquake showed Japan's impressive resilience against mega-earthquakes, it also revealed with hindsight a shocking unpreparedness against the hazards of tsunami and a dangerous negligence with regard to the protection of nuclear power plants against such hazards. Also, the nuclear disaster 240 km North of the Tokyo, once more drew attention to the fact that the extreme regional concentration of economic activity and government functions in Japan's capital strongly increases the vulnerability of the country to mega disasters. All these issues need to be continuously addressed and analyzed. Obstacles to their resolution are likely to be rooted in socio-psychological conditions as well as in governance deficiencies caused by characteristics of Japan's politico-economic system. But these are questions beyond the scope of this book. However, third, the framework for the evaluation and management of systemic risk outlined in Chap. 6 can provide orientation to detect and resolve governance deficiencies. The framework not only addresses the fundamental epistemic issues with regard to the evaluation of mega disasters, it also emphasizes the need to move beyond closed circles of expert knowledge in order to deal with the ambiguities involved in the analysis of systemic risks, to gain wider public awareness and to achieve political consensus about necessary counter-measures.

References

Bank of Japan (2018) Flow of funds. Overview of Japan, the United States and the Euro Area. https://www.boj.or.jp/en/statistics/sj/sjhiq.pdf. Last accessed 14 Jan 2019

Cabinet Office (2017) *保険・共済による災害への備えの促進に関する検討会昱告* (Report by the study group related to the promotion of insurance and cooperative insurance for disaster preparedness). http://www.bousai.go.jp/kaigirep/hisaisha_kyosai/index.html. Last Accessed 14 Jan 2019

Hofstede G, Hofstede GJ, Minkove M (2010) Cultures and organizations. Software of the mind. McGraw Hill, New York

Hood M, Kamesaka A, Nofsinger J, Tamura T (2013) Investor response to a natural disaster. Evidence from Japan's 2011 earthquake. Pac Basin Financ J 25:240–252

Kamesaka A (2013) The great east Japan earthquake and investor behavior in Japan's equity markets. Public Policy Rev 8(6):775–790

Kan N (2017) The Fukushima nuclear power plant disaster and the future of renewable energy. Cornell University Press, Ithaca

Munich Re (2019) NatCatService. Earthquake/Tsunami events worldwide 1990–2017. https://natcatservice.munichre.com. Last Accessed 14 Jan 2019

OECD (2015) OECD economic surveys Japan. OECD, Paris

Sompo Risk Management (2017) *平成28年度自然災害時における中小企業の事業継続に関する調査事業昱告書* (Survey report on business continuity planning by small and medium sized enterprises with regard to natural disasters, for the fiscal year 2016). http://www.chusho.meti.go.jp/keiei/antei/2017/170414saigai.pdf. Last accessed 14 Jan 2019

Waldenberger F (2013) Confronting earthquake risk in Japan—are private households underinsured? Eur Asia J 11(1):78–91

Waldenberger F, Eilker J (2012) Das Tohoku Erdbeben—wirtschaftliche Auswirkungen (the economic impact of the Tokoku earthquake). In: Chiavacci D, Wieczorek I (eds) Japan Jahrbuch 2011. VSJF, Berlin, pp 187–226

World Bank (2019) The World Bank data indicators. Land area. https://data.worldbank.org/indicator. Last accessed 14 Jan 2019

Chapter 2
Japan's Disaster Risk Financing: Framework and Policies

Takahiro Tsuda

Abstract Throughout its history, Japan has faced various types of natural disasters, including the Great East Japan Earthquake in 2011. Against this backdrop, the country has developed a wide range of country-specific disaster risk financing (DRF) tools, and encouraged developing countries to follow suit. This chapter is the first attempt to capture the key characteristics of Japan's own DRF tools and the cross-border DRF policies for development purposes. Specifically, Japan's earthquake insurance, established in 1966, provides a means of burden-sharing between the public and private sectors through a three-tiered system. The government also tailors its budgetary schemes to various recovery and reconstruction needs, in accordance with the magnitude and characteristics of the disasters. Lastly, the chapter discusses sovereign risk pools and bilateral development loans, both as disaster countermeasures.

1 Introduction

The Great East Japan Earthquake in 2011 was one of many reminders that Japan is a disaster-prone country. According to the official statistics, the earthquake and subsequent tsunami resulted in 15,894 fatalities, as well as 2,546 people missing, and 6,156 injured.[1] In addition, more than 120,000 buildings were completely destroyed and some major roads and railways collapsed, cutting lifelines for local residents. The recovery is still ongoing.

The events of 2011 are not new. Throughout its history, Japan has faced various types of natural disasters, including earthquakes, tsunamis, typhoons, and volcanoes, all of which resulted in a great number of human lives being lost, key infrastructure being destroyed, and social and business activities being damaged. For instance, in

[1]National Police Agency, December 8, 2017.

T. Tsuda (✉)
Office of Planning and Coordination for International Affairs, International Bureau, Ministry of Finance, Tokyo, Japan
e-mail: takahiro.tsuda@mof.go.jp

A. Kamesaka and F. Waldenberger (eds.), *Governance, Risk and Financial Impact of Mega Disasters*, Economics, Law, and Institutions in Asia Pacific,
https://doi.org/10.1007/978-981-13-9005-0_2

the Great Kanto Earthquake of 1923, one of the largest natural disasters experienced in the country, the death toll totaled 142,807 people, most of whom were killed in fire incidents. The Fukui Earthquake of 1948 caused the deaths of more than 5,000 people and the Great Hanshin–Awaji Earthquake of 1995 killed more than 6,000 people. Moreover, even today, the risk of future disasters remains imminent: for instance, there are 110 active volcanoes in Japan, which accounts for more than 7% of all the active volcanoes throughout the globe in 2014.

In the face of these challenges, Japan has developed various disaster risk management (DRM) tools, along with corresponding financing measures. However, there has been no attempt to conduct a comprehensive analysis of Japan's disaster risk financing (DRF) framework.[2] This chapter is the first attempt to discuss the key characteristics of DRF tools in Japan as of mid 2018. Specifically, it provides a broad overview of Japan's DRF tools, and of its bilateral and multilateral tools that assist developing partners to prepare DRF policies.

This chapter is divided into five sections. The first section reviews the basic frameworks for DRM and DRF in Japan. In Sects. 2 and 3, we discuss two of Japan's DRF tools, earthquake insurance and the budgetary response to earthquakes. The Ministry of Finance, as the fiscal authority, plays a central role in these tools by designing the policy framework. Then, Sect. 4 reviews the cross-border DRF tools provided by the Japanese government, targeted at assisting countries with a limited capacity to cope with disasters. Section 5 summarizes the findings and discusses some implications and future issues.

2 Basic Frameworks for DRM and DRF in Japan

Before discussing the DRF framework, it is useful to describe Japan's overall DRM framework and strategy, as DRF is a critical component of the country's national DRM framework (see OECD 2012; Clarke and Dercon 2016). Japan's DRM structure was first established when the *Disaster Countermeasures Basic Act* was enacted in 1961, following a series of typhoons in 1959. The Act requires the central and prefectural governments to produce national and regional disaster management plans, respectively. The national plan comprehensively sets out three different stages of policy responses, comprising (i) prevention, (ii) emergency response, and (iii) restoration and reconstruction (Government of Japan 1963).[3] The greatest emphasis is placed on the prevention stage, based on the concept that prevention is the best way to safeguard the lives and properties of citizens.[4] Below, we examine each stage in order.

[2] Although global and regional surveys exist (OECD 2013, 2015), they lack in-depth investigations of country-specific circumstances.

[3] The national plan elaborates on the characteristics of these three policy responses for 15 different types of disasters, including both natural and man-made disasters, as well as features that are common to all disasters.

[4] See Articles 1 and 35 of the *Disaster Countermeasures Basic Act*.

Prevention. At the *prevention* stage, the government is committed to preparing a set of policy menus. The first set of policies makes disaster prevention a priority in urban planning, builds infrastructure that is resilient to potential disasters, and ensures that lifeline facilities are fully functional. Such activities aim to directly mitigate the impact of future disasters.

The government is also committed to raising awareness, providing necessary training, and promoting knowledge sharing, on the grounds that the number of casualties from disasters can be greatly reduced when populations are well prepared. Various preparatory measures, such as assigning lead authorities, determining their cooperation arrangements, and safeguarding adequate resources, are included in the plan. Moreover, the plan requires the government to enhance research and analysis on the magnitude and probability of potential disasters because ensuring an adequate risk assessment capacity is indispensable in successful DRM.

Emergency response. An *emergency response* must be provided immediately after any disaster. The national plan elaborates a possible order of emergency responses, including immediate alerts, evacuation, rescue activities, and the provision of living support (supplies of food, medical services, and shelter). Further, the respective roles of different organizations—various ministries at the national level, local governments, and the private sector—are specified in detail in the plan. The emphasis is placed on how to secure accurate information flows, given that post-disaster turmoil may compromise proper decision-making based on facts and data.

Recovery and reconstruction. The emergency operation is followed by *recovery and reconstruction* actions, which may extend over many years and which include the restoration of infrastructure, transportation, and basic institutions, as well as ensuring credit lines to small and medium-sized enterprises. The plan spells out the necessary steps to recover the viability of the regional economy and requires the government to provide an enabling environment for business developments and urban planning, as well as access to social welfare and education.

Although the national plan itself does not elaborate the DRF scheme in detail, we can map out the domestic DRF tools by matching them to each stage of the DRM framework, as shown in Fig. 1.[5] In line with DRM, DRF makes prevention (risk mitigation and reduction) a priority (World Bank Group 2019).

First, at the prevention stage, the government uses its ordinary budget to implement various DRM measures, such as building infrastructure that is resilient to potential future disasters. When building the infrastructure, a comprehensive cost–benefit analysis is undertaken, examining the cash flows for the entire life of the projects, including not only upfront construction costs but also maintenance and repair costs.

[5]The Director-General for Disaster Management in the Cabinet Office, a central government hub for DRM, secures a certain amount of its own budget for DRM (6.2 billion yen for FY2018). However, this budget item does not encompass all the spending on the DRF tools. DRF expenditure on items such as financing sources for resilient infrastructure and contingency reserves are outside this budget.

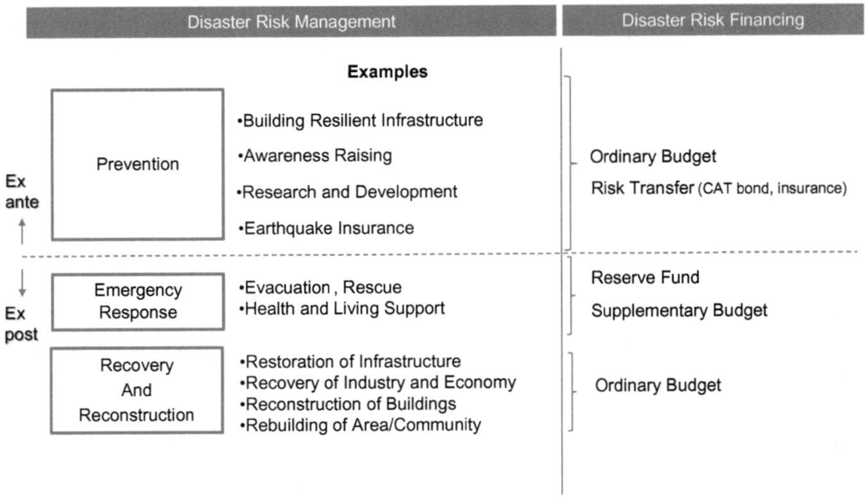

Fig. 1 Conceptual framework for DRM and DRF. *Source* Author

Then, there are a wide variety of DRF tools used to finance the emergency measures. For instance, both the national and local governments use their respective accumulated reserves.[6] Every year, the national government sets aside "disaster recovery expenditure" in addition to the general contingency reserve that can be used for various purposes (for the general reserve, see Box 1). Often, the disaster recovery expenditure in the initial budget is not sufficient to cover all the natural disasters, and supplementary budgets must be formulated.[7] In addition to the national government's efforts, local governments tend to accumulate reserves that are specifically dedicated to both disaster prevention and recovery.[8]

Alternatively, the government can formulate a supplementary budget that will need to be passed in the Diet, without resorting to its annual reserves. Such supplementary budgets can be financed by temporary taxes, the issuance of bonds, the reallocation of other budget items, or a combination of these. The government could resort to emergency credit lines from international partners, but such an option is less likely given that Japan is an advanced economy.

[6]As it must be accumulated well before a disaster, the reserve can be categorized as an ex ante measure. See OECD (2012).

[7]For instance, from FY2013–FY2017, on average, the amount of disaster recovery expenditure in the initial budget was 73,261 million yen, whereas that in the supplementary budget was 214,052 million yen.

[8]See http://www.soumu.go.jp/iken/h28_118776.html (in Japanese only).

Finally, at the recovery and reconstruction stage, fiscal support needs to be secured through ordinary budgets, given its medium-term nature. The total budget for disaster countermeasures cannot be determined, as it is spread out among different budget areas, such as infrastructure investment, education, social security, agriculture, and so on.

Apart from government financing, the private sector plays a role in preparing post-disaster expenditure. An example is the issuance of catastrophe bonds (CAT bonds), in which bondholders receive a higher interest rate but must give up repayment of the bond's principal when a contractually predetermined type of catastrophe occurs. Effectively, the issuance of CAT bonds enables the issuer to transfer the risk to investors. CAT bonds are becoming common in Japan, as information in the press suggested that the total issuance amount totaled 220 billion yen in February 2016.[9] One example is the MUTEKI bonds, which are CAT bonds issued by the Japan Agriculture (JA) mutual aid system and which resulted in 100% loss of the principal immediately after the Great East Japan earthquake in 2011. The investors' loss meant a parallel benefit to the issuer (i.e., JA), which then used the proceeds for payments to insured farmers.

Box 1: Use of the general contingency reserve

Each year, the national government establishes a 250–350 billion yen contingency reserve in the general account. It is used for unexpected expenditure, including responses to disasters such as earthquakes or floods. Examples of other items for which the reserve is used include (i) preventing domestic animal infectious diseases, (ii) organizing by-elections, (iii) filling gaps in lawsuit costs, and (iv) urgent responses to national and international security issues.

Because the money is not ring-fenced for disaster response, there is always a risk that there will not be sufficient money left when a disaster occurs. Historical records suggest that the money has been sufficient to cover disaster-related expenses, partly because the government tends to use other DRF tools (such as the supplementary budget) to cover damages.

[9]Nikkei Shimbun, February 8, 2016.

(billion JPY)

	Disaster-related expenses	Other expenses
FY2010	67.8 • Response to the Great East Japan Earthquake	97.1 • Control for domestic animal infectious diseases
FY2011	63.3 • Response to the Great East Japan Earthquake • Disposal of disaster waste after heavy rainfall • Removal of snow after heavy snow	11.5 • Additional lawsuit costs
FY2012	6.2 • Response to the flood in northern Kyushu district and the typhoon	107.0 • General election by the dissolution of the House of Representatives
FY2013	–	25.4 • Prevention of leakage of polluted water
FY2014	44.8 • Agricultural support against heavy snow	123.5 • General election by the dissolution of the House of Representatives

Note Fiscal Year starts in April and ends the following March
Source Author, based on the Ministry of Finance sources

3 Earthquake Insurance

3.1 Origin

As mentioned in the Introduction, Japan is a country beset by earthquakes. Figure 2 presents a history of earthquakes that resulted in casualties of more than 5,000 people, with the oldest case going back to 1293. One of the worst earthquakes was the Great Kanto Earthquake in 1923, which resulted in 142,000 casualties. Further, as Japan is located at the junction of four tectonic plates, it is anticipated that it could face another massive scale earthquake along the Nankai Trough and severe related disasters in the near future.[10]

Against this backdrop, the need for earthquake insurance has been advocated for a long time in Japan. In 1878, a German professor, Dr. Myett, proposed a nationally

[10]For instance, the government earthquake investigation committee estimates that the likelihood of a potential massive Nankai Trough earthquake in the next 30 years ranges from 70 to 80% (Headquarters for Earthquake Research Promotion 2018).

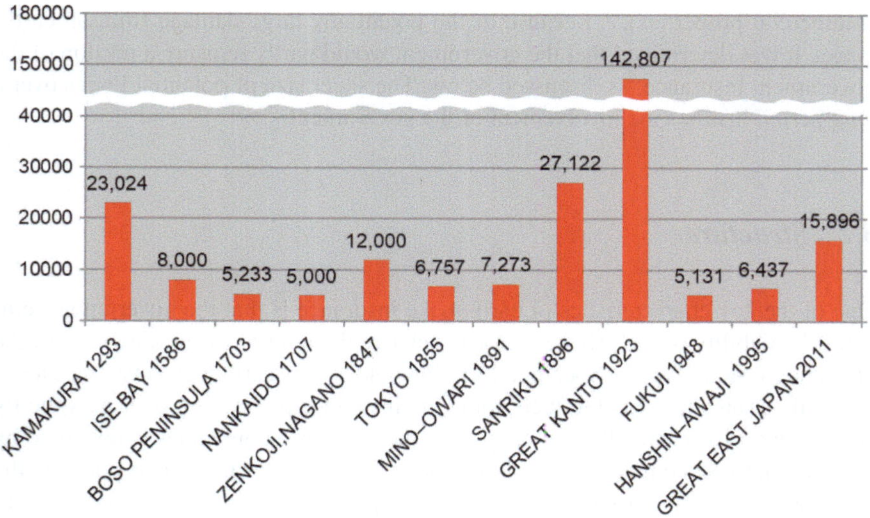

Fig. 2 Number of casualties in earthquakes. *Sources* Reproduced from NGDC/WDS (2018), Cabinet Office Japan (2018), and National Police Agency (2018)

organized earthquake insurance system, but did not obtain sufficient support from the Japanese government or industry. The hesitation arose for the following three reasons: (i) it is difficult to apply the law of large numbers to earthquakes, given the low frequency of incidents compared to other natural disasters; (ii) the cost of the damage can be prohibitively high and it may be difficult to cover it through insurance; and (iii) adverse selection may be difficult to avoid (General Insurance Rate Organization of Japan (GIROJ) 2014).

However, a series of earthquakes in the first half of the twentieth century pushed the government and industry to reconsider earthquake insurance. Although not officially discussed in the Diet, the government proposed a draft earthquake insurance scheme in 1934 and 1949, and the private sector initiated its own study from 1952.

An industry group had just established an expert committee for further investigation of the earthquake insurance system when the Niigata earthquake of 1964 occurred. It caused 26 deaths, with 447 people injured, and the destruction of 1,960 residences. Following this incident, the then Minister of Finance Kakuei Tanaka, who was originally from the earthquake-hit Niigata prefecture, consulted with the Ministry's insurance council to consider a concrete policy response to possible future earthquakes. After a two-year deliberation in the council, the first earthquake insurance scheme was established in 1966.

The primary objective of the earthquake insurance was to bring back stability to victims' lives. Thus, it covered residential buildings and households only (i.e., not commercial properties).[11] Because of the potentially large damage from an earthquake, it was determined that the government would partly reinsure a portion of the government insurance, as discussed below. The sheer size of potential losses over a long period justifies the involvement of the government.

3.2 Structure

One of the key characteristics of earthquake insurance is that the government reinsures the liability of the private sector to achieve the long-term sustainability of the insurance system (Fig. 3). Specifically, policyholders buy earthquake insurance automatically as an attachment to their home fire insurance policy, unless they explicitly decline to do so. Then, all the money from the insurance companies is reinsured by a special purpose company, Japan Earthquake Reinsurance (JER). JER pools all the insurance premiums across the country and keeps part of the money, while distributing portions to the government and the private sector, effectively distributing risks to relevant parties.[12]

The premium rate is determined by the General Insurance Rate Organization of Japan (GIROJ), an industry group that is mandated to calculate and provide a

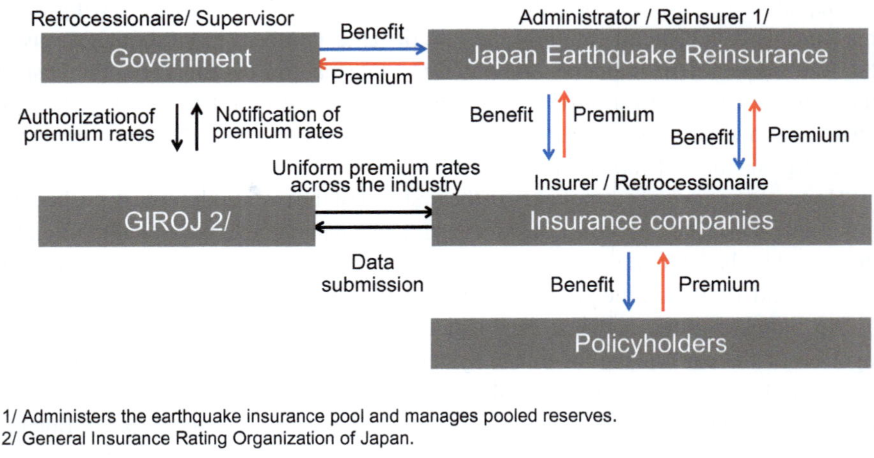

Fig. 3 Overview of the earthquake insurance scheme. *Source* Author, based on the Ministry of Finance

[11]Over time, earthquake insurance has expanded its coverage, such that the current earthquake insurance can be viewed as akin to property insurance (Earthquake Insurance Project Team 2012).

[12]The shares of the government, JER, and the private sector are 78%, 20%, and 2%, respectively.

reference insurance rate to member companies.[13] As far as the earthquake insurance is concerned, the premium rate is set uniformly by the GIROJ and needs to be approved by the Financial Services Agency. Box 2 summarizes the key characteristics of the earthquake insurance scheme.

Box 2: Summary of earthquake insurance

- **Insurance coverage**: Residential buildings and household goods
- **Method of contract**: In principle, automatically attached to fire insurance policy (automatic offer, attached if not rejected by the insured)
- **Loss to be indemnified**: Loss or damage through fire, destruction, burying or washing away caused directly or indirectly by any earthquake or volcanic eruption, or resulting tsunami

Total loss: 100% of insured amount
Large half loss: 60% of insured amount
Small half loss: 30% of insured amount
Partial loss: 5% of insured amount

- **Insurable proportion**: Between 30 and 50% of the fire insurance policy
- **Limit of insured amount**: Residential buildings: JPY 50 million, household goods: JPY 10 million
- **Aggregate limit of indemnity**: JPY 11.3 trillion per earthquake, shared between the private sector (JPY 0.17 trillion) and the government (JPY 11.13 trillion).

Earthquake insurance coverage as an option automatically attached to fire insurance was introduced in 1980, with a view to addressing adverse selection. In addition, the intention was to encourage private insurance companies to promote the use of earthquake insurance because profit-maximizing firms would not otherwise actively sell such insurance (Earthquake Insurance Project Team 2012). However, the introduction of the automatic attachment policy did not significantly alter the market penetration rate during the 1980s or early 1990s (Fig. 4). While the exact reason for this initial low uptake rate is unclear, the penetration rate did improve after the Great Hanshin–Awaji Earthquake in 1995 and the Great East Japan Earthquake in 2011, as the general public was forced, painfully, to realize the necessity of the insurance.

[13]Currently, the insurance rate is from 0.068 to 0.363%, depending on the risk of the area and whether buildings are fireproof. There is a discount if the residence is deemed resilient to earthquakes. Long-term policies also receive a preferable treatment in relation to the premium.

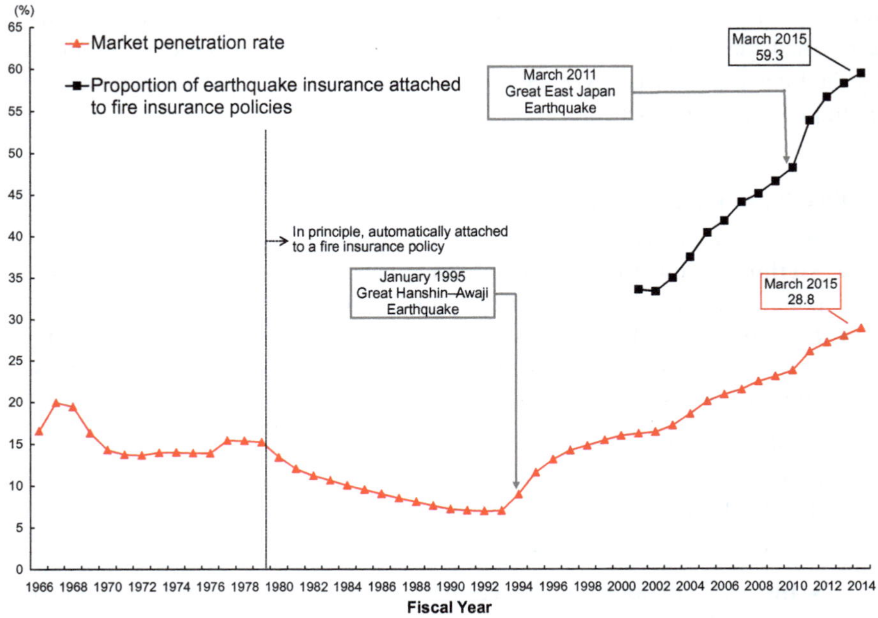

Fig. 4 Market penetration rate. *Source* Author, based on Ministry of Finance documents

3.3 Three-Tiered Burden-Sharing System

The aggregate insured amount is determined based on a potential large-scale earthquake of the same magnitude as the Great Kanto Earthquake (1923). Currently, it is set at 11,300 billion yen, or around 2% of GDP.[14]

Although the JER distributes *insurance premiums* between the government and private insurance companies, another question is how the *burden of payments* for earthquake insurance claims is shared between the two parties. The Japanese government introduced a tiered system, under which the greater is the damage from an earthquake, the higher is the responsibility of the public sector. The underlying idea was to strike the best balance between the principle of insurance and fiscal support: If the loss is manageable, the law of large numbers indicates that the loss should be fully covered by the private sector only, which matches benefits paid and premiums as a whole. Conversely, if the loss is so large that insurance companies cannot bear it by themselves, government intervention is justified.

More specifically, Japan's earthquake insurance scheme introduces a three-tiered burden-sharing system (Fig. 5):

- The first tier involves the private sector only covering the burden;
- The second tier involves the private and public sectors equally sharing the burden; and

[14]If the damage exceeds this limit, extra fiscal support may be considered on a case-by-case basis.

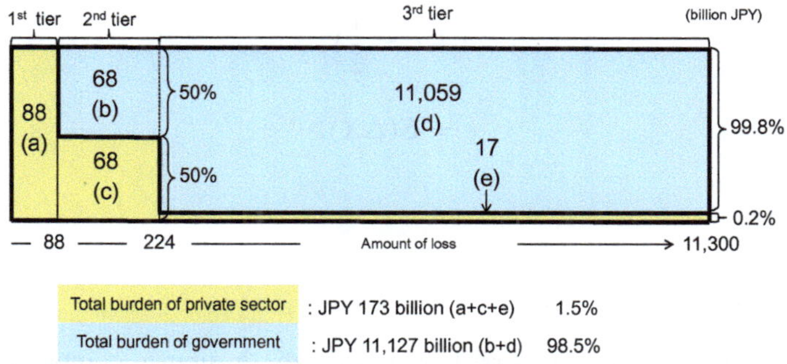

Fig. 5 Structure of burden–sharing between private and public sectors. *Source* Ministry of Finance

– The third tier involves most of the loss being covered by the public sector.

The exact threshold for each tier that triggers liability is carefully determined to ensure that the private sector's burden does not exceed its capacity, but also to ensure that the private sector burden is not too low because excessive government assistance may create a moral hazard. Thus, under the first tier ("(a)" in Fig. 5), the loss amount covered, 88 billion yen, is double the amount of annual premium payments, meaning that the private sector should at least cover earthquake-related costs up to twice the amount of the insurance companies' annual income. Then, the private sector's burden in the first and second tiers combined ("(a)" and "(c)" in Fig. 5) is determined by half the amount of the outstanding stocks of reserves held by the private sector, which is 156 billion yen. Because the private sector's burden is set as half of its reserves, it can retain sufficient absorbing capacity if another earthquake occurs. In the second tier, the public and private sectors split their burden in half (68 billion yen each). Thus, the threshold for the third tier is calculated as 224 billion (the sum of the first and second tiers). In the third tier, the private sector's burden ("(e)" in Fig. 5) is confined to the expected increase of the reserves, so that the private sector reserves (stocks) do not decrease.

To summarize, (a), (b), and (c) are calculated based on the following formula:

$$a = 2X,$$

$$a + c = \frac{1}{2}Y,$$

$$e = E(\Delta X),$$

where

X *Premium (flow)*
Y *Reserve (stock)*.

The reasons for setting the first tier at twice the insurance companies' annual income or for establishing the private sector's burden in the first and second tiers combined as equal to half the amount of the reserves are matters of policy judgment. For instance, before the Great East Japan Earthquake in 2011, the formula above were set as follows:

$$a + c = Y$$

$$e = 2E(\Delta X)$$

After 2011, the liability of the private sector exceeded the total reserves, which dropped sharply post-disaster from around 1.0 trillion (February 2011) to 0.5 trillion (March 2012) because of large-scale payments to the victims of the earthquake and subsequent tsunami. Thus, revisions were made in May 2013 to alter the formula to its current version and eliminate the excess liability of the private sector (Figs. 6 and 7).

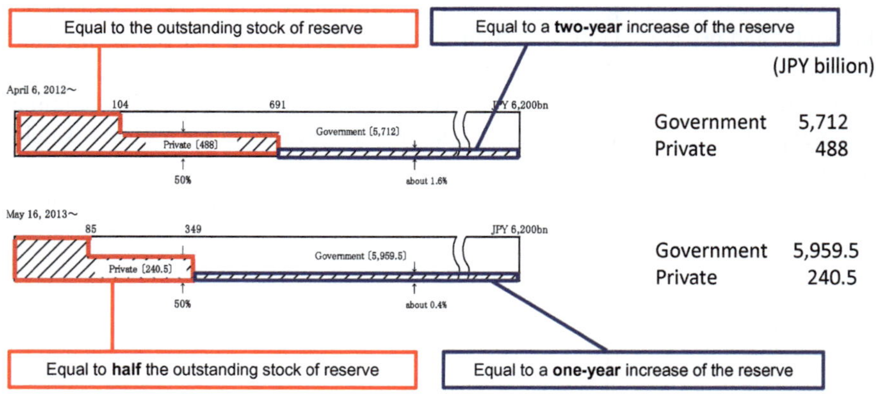

Fig. 6 Revision after the Great East Japan earthquake. *Source* Author, based on Ministry of Finance

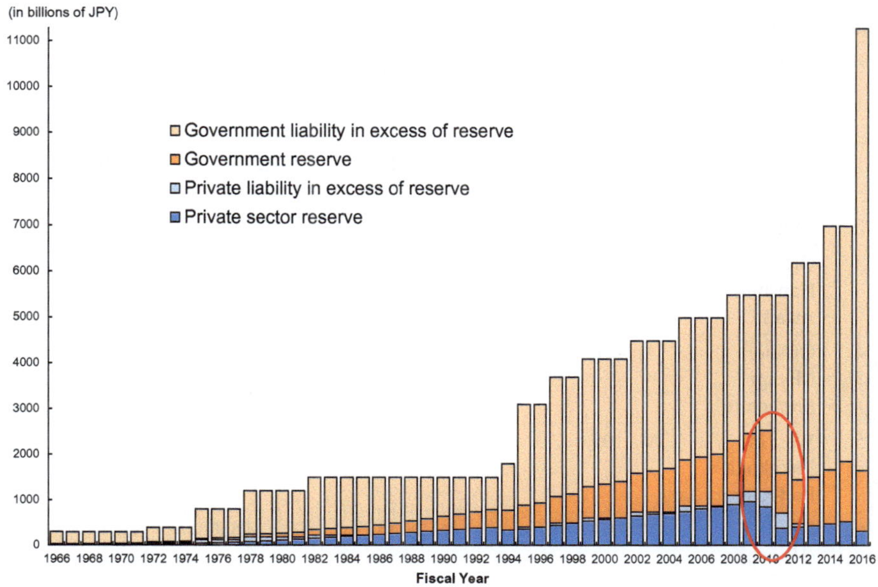

Fig. 7 Evolution of liability and reserves. *Source* Author, based on Ministry of Finance

3.4 Activation Record

The government payment (i.e., the second and third tiers) has not been used for all the earthquakes, but it was activated for the Great Hanshin–Awaji (1995), Great East Japan (2011), and Kumamoto (2016) Earthquakes. The limited number of cases in which government payments have been activated, despite a series of large-scale earthquakes, may suggest that the coverage of the earthquake insurance is not wide enough in earthquake-hit areas.[15] This question needs to be explored further in future research (Table 1).

4 Fiscal Framework for Recovery and Reconstruction from Earthquakes

This section examines the fiscal framework that is employed for reconstruction following large earthquakes. By investigating three examples—the Great Hanshin–Awaji Earthquake in 1995, the Great East Japan Earthquake in 2011, and the recent

[15]For instance, the penetration rate of Hyogo prefecture, which was the most severely affected by the Great Hanshin–Awaji Earthquake, was 4.8% in FY1994, compared to the then-national average of 9.0%.

Table 1 Past ten major earthquakes and activation of government payments

	Earthquake	Date	Magnitude	Number of policies	Claim paid	
					(JPY Billion)	Paid for government
1	Great East Japan	Mar-11	9.0	807,152	1,274.9	580
2	Kumamoto	Apr-16	7.3	200,029	375.3	130
3	Great Hanshin–Awaji	Jan-95	7.3	65,427	78.3	6.2
4	Offshore Miyagi Prefecture	Apr-11	7.2	31,005	32.4	–
5	West of Fukukoka Prefecture	Mar-05	7.0	22,066	17.0	–
6	Geiyo (Hiroshima and Ehime Prefectures)	Mar-01	6.7	24,452	16.9	–
7	Mid Niigata Prefectures (2014)	Oct-04	6.8	12,608	14.9	–
8	Mid Niigata Prefectures (2007)	Jul-07	6.8	7,869	8.2	–
9	Western Offshore Fukukoka Prefecture	Apr-05	5.8	11,337	6.4	–
10	Offshore Tokachi (Hokkaido Prefecture)	Sep-03	8.0	10,553	6.0	–

Source Ministry of Finance

Kumamoto Earthquake in April 2016—the section illustrates how Japan tailors different fiscal tools to different cases, depending on the damage and duration of the post-disaster impact.

4.1 Great Hanshin–Awaji Earthquake (1995)

The Great Hanshin–Awaji Earthquake occurred in January 1995 and resulted in 6,437 casualties. Immediately after the earthquake, the government formulated a supplementary budget for the emergency response (including the rescue operation) and restoration of lifelines, which amounted to more than one trillion yen. In the next fiscal year, other large-scale supplementary budgets were prepared to cover immediate needs, including the restoration of infrastructures such as public schools and medical care facilities. In addition, the government began to include, in its ordinary initial budgets, an amount for ongoing annual recovery costs, which were used for costs such as support for small and medium-sized enterprises, disaster countermeasures, employment support, and to build resilient cities. The sizes of both the initial budgets and supplementary budgets were reduced over time, reflecting the progress of the recovery.

In the end, the total expenditure for emergency aid, restoration, and reconstruction amounted to 5,020 billion yen in total (roughly 1% of GDP at the time). Nearly 77% of the financing resources came from the recurring supplementary budgets (Fig. 8).

Historically, Japan has relied on supplementary budgets every year for various purposes, such as stimulus packages, responses to disasters, and urgent needs to enhance the national defense capacity. Hence, the active use of supplementary budgets itself was not special. What was notable was the accelerated implementation of the emergency and recovery operation, as suggested by the size of the supplementary budgets in FY1995, which accounted for more than 40% of the total package.

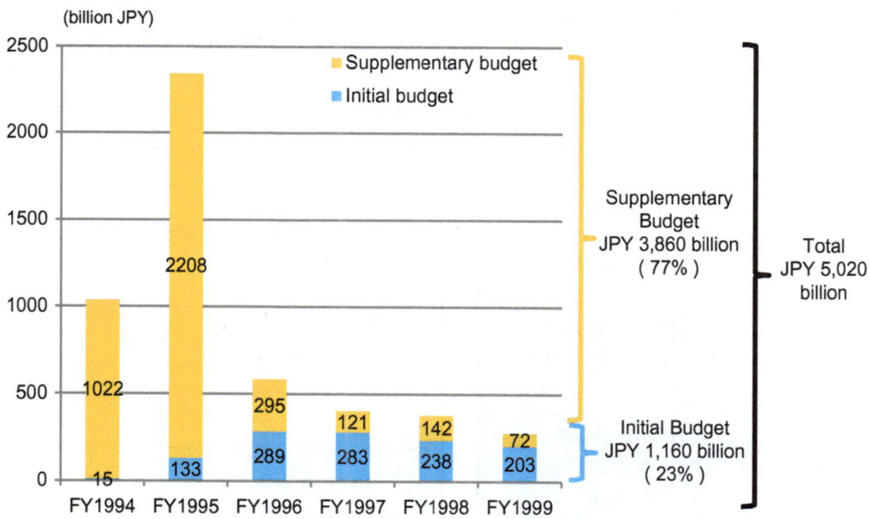

Fig. 8 Financing of the reconstruction after the Great Hanshin–Awaji Earthquake. *Source* Author, based on Ministry of Finance

4.2 Great East Japan Earthquake (2011)

The Great East Japan Earthquake and the subsequent tsunami resulted in a devastating amount of damage. The government concluded that merely combining the supplementary budgets and increasing ordinary budgets would be insufficient as a fiscal response. Therefore, in April 2012, a special account (the *Special Account for Reconstruction from the Great East Japan Earthquake*) was established, with a view to ring-fencing revenue and expenditure for the purpose of reconstruction from the ordinary budgeting process under the general account.

The revenue in this special account came from special taxes and bond issuances and the expenditure it covered included reconstruction project costs and redemption of reconstruction bonds (Fig. 9). The special taxes comprised personal income tax (+2.1%), corporate tax (+10%, until its expiry in FY2013), and local residence tax (JPY 1,000).

One peculiar aspect of this special account is that it was designed as a temporary account. Initially, the framework was established for a period of five years, based on the assumption that the reconstruction could be largely completed within that

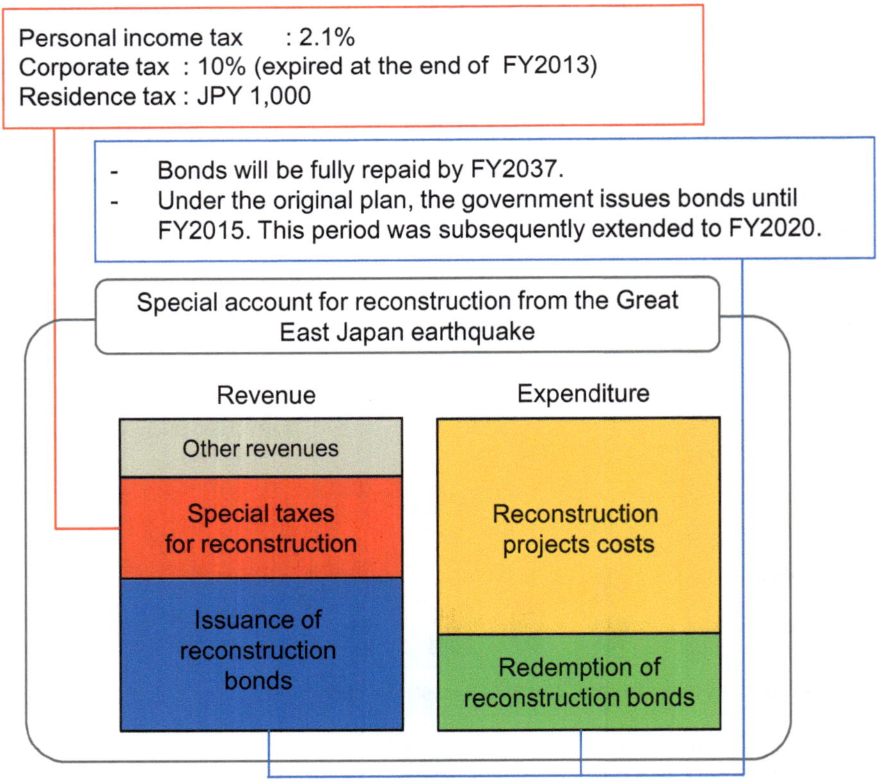

Fig. 9 Overview of the special account for reconstruction. *Source* Author

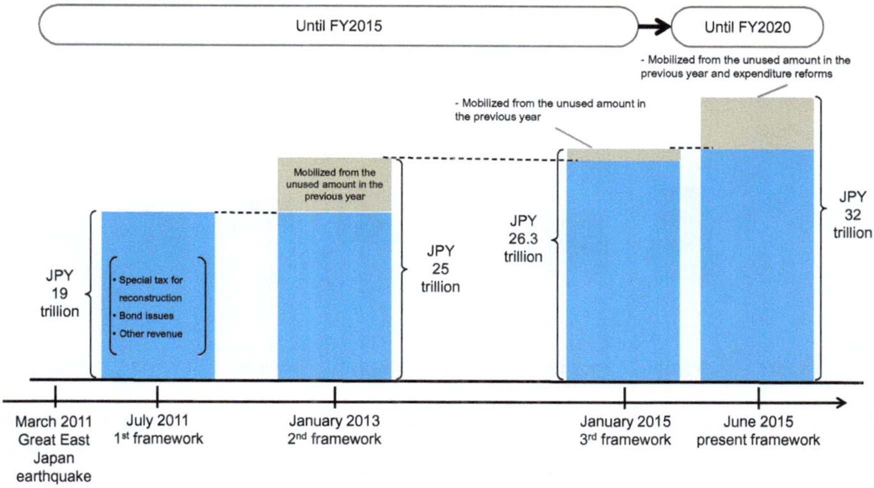

Fig. 10 Evolution of the size of the reconstruction special account. *Source* Author

time frame. The bond repayment and issuance schedule, as well as the temporary tax hike, were meant to finish after five years (i.e., by FY2015), with the size of the total package being 19 trillion yen. However, over time, the size of the reconstruction package was increased, rising to 25 trillion in January 2013 and then 26.3 trillion in January 2015. Before the end of the planned five-year period, in June 2015, the government decided to extend the framework over another five years to FY2020, and increased funds to 32 trillion yen in total.

This series of gradual increases in the size of the reconstruction project suggests that there was strong pressure for increased expenditure from line ministries. Further, the extension of the recovery and reconstruction period indicates that the recovery and reconstruction are taking a much longer time than was originally planned (Fig. 10).

It should be noted that the bond issuance was used as a tool to accelerate the expenditure. In the first year, revenue from issuing reconstruction bonds was used for project costs and then, using the special tax revenue (and, to a lesser extent, transfers from a general account), the debt was repaid in the following years (Fig. 11). In other words, the bond issuance scheme allowed the government to accelerate implementation of reconstruction projects by relying on future tax increases.

4.3 Kumamoto Earthquake (2016)

While the impact of the Kumamoto Earthquake was huge, the expected expenditure on fiscal support was not as large as that following the Great East Japan Earthquake. As an initial response, the government formulated a supplementary budget of 778 billion yen, tapping into unused money (mainly by reducing the interest payment

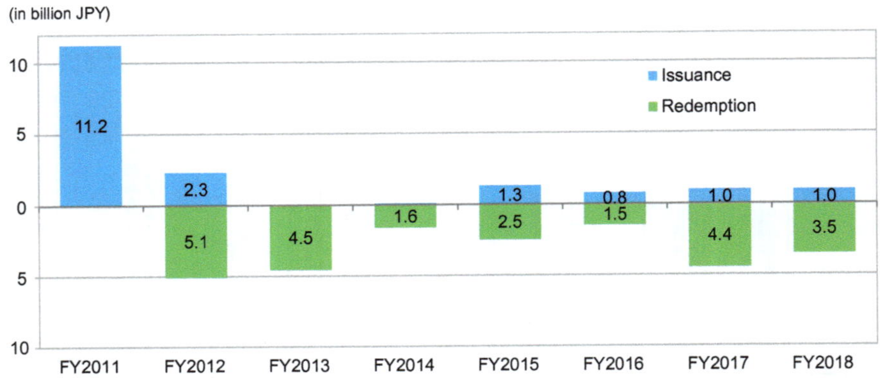

Fig. 11 Issuance and redemption schedule of reconstruction bonds. *Source* Author. *Note* Figures in FY2011–FY2016 are settled figures; Figures in FY2017 are based on the supplementary budget; figures in FY2018 are based on the initial budget.

expenditure). As the memory of the Great East Japan Earthquake remained vivid, expenditure pressure from the line ministries was high. However, the government carefully assessed the immediate impact, and avoided unnecessary increase in expenditure.

4.4 Summary

The Japanese government tailors various fiscal tools to case-specific circumstances, in particular the fiscal requirements and severity of the earthquake in question. This is demonstrated by its use of supplementary budgets (Great Hanshin–Awaji Earthquake), a dedicated special account framework (Great East Japan Earthquake), and reallocation of expenditure (Kumamoto Earthquake). In the case of the Great East Japan Earthquake, the government employed reconstruction bonds as a tool to accelerate recovery and reconstruction by relying on future tax revenue. As a general lesson, fiscal authorities need to carefully assess the necessity and the extent of increasing budgets in response to requests from line ministries. In addition, it is essential to expedite reconstruction and prevent a prolonged reconstruction period in the long run.

5 Japan's Efforts to Promote DRF in the International Arena

As discussed in the previous sections, Japan has a full suite of DRM measures to tackle domestic disasters. In addition, it prioritizes disaster countermeasures in the international diplomacy and development spheres. For instance, Japan led the discussion in setting international standards on DRM in forums such as the Hyogo Framework for Action (2005) and the Sendai Framework for Disaster Risk Reduction (2015). Further, in 2014, the Japanese government committed US$ 1 million to the Japan–World Bank Program for Mainstreaming Disaster Risk Management in Developing Countries, and helped establish the World Bank Tokyo DRM Hub, the mandate of which is to extend Japanese and global expertise in DRM to developing countries through sharing of knowledge and country-based programs.[16]

Financial protection is one of the key elements of resilience, as highlighted by the Sendai Framework. Thus, our next question is whether Japan is equipped with sufficient DRF tools to support its strong leadership in DRM. This section reviews Japan's efforts to provide DRF to international partners, at both pre-disaster and post-disaster stages.

For the pre-disaster stage, Japan promotes resilient infrastructure in its bilateral and multilateral assistance programs. In March 2015, Japan announced the Sendai Cooperation Initiative for Disaster Risk Reduction (DRR), which aims at mainstreaming DRR in all development policies and planning. One of the pillars of this initiative is investment in DRR from the long-term perspective, noting that prior investment in DRR is more cost effective than post-disaster emergency response and recovery and that it contributes to sustainable development. Based on this idea, the Japanese government was committed to providing US$ 4 billion assistance and capacity building for 40,000 people from 2015 to 2018 in its official development assistance program. The government envisages that mobilizing financial resources to develop resilient infrastructure will assist in incentivizing developing partners to pay more attention to DRM.

For the post-disaster stage, Japan's initiatives include both bilateral and multilateral assistance. In regard to DRF tools for bilateral assistance, the Japan International Cooperation Agency has specific disaster-related emergency assistance programs, ranging from dispatching experts to providing living support.[17] During 1987–2017, 144 emergency response teams, which included rescue, medical, pandemic, self-defense, and other personnel, were dispatched. Living support has been provided in 511 cases for 43 disaster-hit countries and areas (as of June 2017). Grants are available for either governments or international organizations that are engaged in rescue operations in disaster-hit areas.

Further, in April 2013, the Japanese government created a new menu of bilateral assistance, called Stand-by Emergency Credit for Urgent Recovery, or SECURE. Under SECURE, the requesting country can seal an exchange of notes and loan agreement well before a disaster, so that loan disbursement for immediate needs can be expedited based on declaration of a trigger, with minimal post-disaster paperwork. By the end of 2017, SECURE had been used by Peru (US$ 10 billion worth of assistance), El Salvador (US$ 5 billion), and the Philippines (US$ 50 billion).

[16]As of November 2017, the program had provided technical assistance worth US$ 58 million and facilitated US$ 2 billion worth of World Bank loans.

[17]Under this program, "disaster" is defined as including both natural and man-made disasters, but not conflicts.

The Japanese government is a pioneer in promoting DRF in multilateral forums, particularly in establishing regional risk pools. For instance, Japan provided a grant for a World Bank study investigating the establishment of a risk pool in the Caribbean region in 2015. Such regional risk pools have multidimensional benefits, such as diversifying risks, establishing joint reserves, transferring excess risks, sharing operational costs, and building a better foundation of risk information (World Bank Group 2017). Japan's initiative in this regard attracted support from other donor countries and culminated in the establishment of the first multi-country catastrophe risk pool, the Caribbean Catastrophe Risk Insurance Facility (CCRIF) in 2007.

Moreover, Japan has taken a leading role in establishing another regional DRF framework for the Pacific Island countries (PICs), the Pacific Catastrophic Risk Assessment and Financing Initiative (PCRAFI). When they are hit by national disasters, most PICs face critical financial challenges. They find it difficult to secure immediate liquidity for swift post-disaster emergency responses without compromising their long-term fiscal balance because they are constrained by their size, borrowing capacity, and limited access to the international insurance market. Against this backdrop, in January 2013, Japan provided financial support to the Secretariat of the Pacific Community and the World Bank, which then jointly started the PCRAFI. Then, other donors such as Germany, the United Kingdom, and the United States participated in this initiative as part of the G7 InsuResilience Global Partnership.[18] The PCRAFI Facility has its insurance contracts partly reinsured with private sector re-insurers so as to partly transfer the risk exposure to market participants.[19]

Japan was involved deeply in designing the PCRAFI scheme. While a special purpose vehicle collects insurance premiums from the insured PICs, during the initial phase of the scheme (2013–2015), the insurance premium was fully subsidized by Japan as additional assistance, except in the case of the Cook Islands. This support facilitated the participation of the insured countries at the initial stage of the scheme, assisting to give the participants a sense of ownership as insurance holders.

These developments were followed by other regional sovereign risk pools, such as the African Risk Capacity, which commenced their first policies in 2014. Currently, if all three existing sovereign risk pools are considered in combination, 27 countries have utilized the regional facilities.[20] These facilities tend to be supplemented with their own technical assistance programs, which serve as knowledge hubs in building catastrophe risk models and accumulating necessary expertise (for more details, see World Bank Group 2017).

---

[18] At the Elmau Summit in 2015, under the German Presidency, the G7 countries set a goal to increase the number of people who have access to direct or indirect insurance coverage against climate hazards in vulnerable developing countries from 100 to 400 million by 2020. By combining "insurance" and "resilience", the initiative was named "InsuResilience".

[19] PCRAFI covers 80% of all losses below a 1-in-20-year event, while transferring the rest of the exposure to reinsurers, 20% of all losses below a 1-in-20-year event and 100% of all losses above a 1-in-20-year event (2016–17 Business Plan).

[20] 16 CCRIF countries (2017/18 policy year), 5 PCRAFI countries (2017/18 policy year), and 6 ARC countries (2016/17 rainfall season).

6 Conclusion

Any government must consider the wise usage of its own DRF tools, which must be based on a comprehensive national DRM system. Japan is not an exception, and it has a wide range of DRF tools that correspond to the different DRM stages, i.e., prevention, emergency, and recovery and reconstruction, in accordance with its *Disaster Countermeasure Basic Act*. Private sector market participants use their own DRF tools, such as insurance and CAT bonds.

Japan's earthquake insurance has been developed based on its long history of recurrent earthquakes. A means of burden-sharing between the public and private sectors is established in a three-tiered system, with due consideration given to the private sector's capacity to pay for the benefits to victims. Improving the market penetration of earthquake insurance held by Japanese citizens should be a further goal.

The government tailors different budgetary schemes to the various disaster-related needs. In accordance with the magnitude and characteristics of the disasters, the fiscal authorities have selected a financing solution that includes aspects such as the use of supplementary budgets, the creation of a special account, or the reallocation of expenditure. The fiscal authorities face challenges in fine-tuning the size and the length of the reconstruction packages, particularly when reconstruction takes longer than originally envisaged.

The Japanese government provides various DRF solutions in the international development area, given its leading role in DRM. In particular, Japan is committed to securing bilateral loans for DRR for 2015–18, and it provides bilateral loans to countries in need in an expeditious manner through disaster response teams or SECURE. It also plays an eminent role in designing DRF solutions on the multilateral front, in particular through establishing regional sovereign risk pools, such as the CCRIF and the PCRAFI. Japan will continue to contribute to global efforts for the development of DRF across the board.

Acknowledgements Takahiro Tsuda is grateful to Hideaki Hamada and Rie Yamaguchi for their invaluable comments. Yusuke Hayashida, Sokichi Morioka, and Shun Sakata provided much-appreciated research assistance. The views and opinions expressed in this article are those of the author and do not necessarily reflect the official policy or position of the Japanese government.

References

Cabinet Office Japan (2018) Bôsai hakusho (White paper on disaster management). http://www.bousai.go.jp/kaigirep/hakusho/h30.html

Clarke DJ, Dercon S (2016) Dull disasters? how planning ahead will make a difference. World Bank Group, Washington, D. C.

Earthquake Insurance Project Team (2012) Jishin hôkenseido ni kansuru purojekutochîmu hôkokusho (Earthquake insurance project team final report). http://www.mof.go.jp/about_mof/councils/jisinpt/report/20121130_00.html

General Insurance Rating Organization of Japan (GIROJ) (2014) Earthquake insurance in Japan. https://www.giroj.or.jp/english/pdf/Earthquake.pdf
Government of Japan (1963) Bôsai kihon keikaku (Basic disaster management plan). www.bousai.go.jp/taisaku/keikaku/pdf/kihon_basic_plan170411.pdf
Headquarters for Earthquake Research Promotion (2018) Chôki hyôka ni yoru jishin hassei kakuritsu-chi no kôshin ni tsuite (Updating of earthquake occurrence through long-term evaluation). https://www.jishin.go.jp/evaluation/long_term_evaluation/chousa_18feb_kakuritsu_index/
National Geophysical Data Center/World Data Service (NGDC/WDS) (2018) Significant earthquake database. National Geophysical Data Center, NOAA. https://www.ngdc.noaa.gov/nndc/struts/form?t=101650&s=1&d=1
National Police Agency (2018) Tôhoku chihô Taiheiyô oki jishin no keisatsu sochi to higai jôkyô (Police measures and the damage situation of the Great East Japan Earthquake). Kōhō shiryō (Public information). 10 Sept. https://www.npa.go.jp/news/other/earthquake2011/pdf/higaijokyo.pdf
Organization for Economic Cooperation and Development (OECD) (2012) Disaster risk assessment and risk financing—a G20/OECD methodological framework. https://www.oecd.org/gov/risk/G20disasterriskmanagement.pdf
Organization for Economic Cooperation and Development (OECD) (2013) Disaster risk financing in APEC economies. https://www.oecd.org/daf/fin/insurance/OECD_APEC_DisasterRiskFinancing.pdf
Organization for Economic Cooperation and Development (OECD) (2015) Disaster risk financing: a global survey of practices and challenges. OECD Publications, Paris
World Bank Group (2017) Sovereign catastrophe risk pools: World Bank technical contribution to the G20. World Bank Group, Washington, D.C.
World Bank Group (2019) Financial risk management of public assets against natural disasters, Japan country case study, Mimeo

Chapter 3
Analysis of the Possible Impact of a Tokyo Mega Earthquake on Japanese Public Finance

Motohiro Sato

In this chapter, I offer an assessment of how a mega earthquake in Tokyo would affect the macroeconomy of Japan and public finance. This is based on a joint research project with Prof. Oguro of Hosei University (Oguro and Sato 2011). Admittedly, a lot of uncertainty is involved in evaluating the impact of a large disaster like a mega earthquake. Even so, quantitative assessment will be of some help to better understand potential risk confronting Japan. The following is a brief description of the research.

This research considers a simple, what we call Keynesian macroeconomic model to quantify the impact of a large-scale earthquake in Tokyo on the macroeconomy. The model includes the macroeconomic variables such as economic growth and inflation, interest rates, as well as fiscal balance and relies on the Monte Carlo simulation method. The result of the simulation reveals the way that these macroeconomic variables change after the earthquake. In Oguro and Sato (2011) the simulations reveal that while GDP falls immediately after the disaster, there will be quick recovery restructuring projects boosting the economy. Overall, the impact of the earthquake on the economy seems to be limited. The reason behind this result is that our staged economy with society aging damps supply decline and increasing macro demand after the disaster with keeping GDP gap modest. The following analysis updates the data from Oguro and Sato (2011).

The simulation is taken from 2015 to 2035 and it is assumed that the earthquake will occur in the year 2020. It can be shown that in the baseline scenario, immediately after the earthquake, whereas the growth rate considerably declines, it picks up relatively quickly due to the post-earthquake recovery investment taken by the government. The overall impact of the earthquake on the macro economy seems to be limited. The result may be surprising but the reason behind this is our long standing stagnant economy with an aging society. This in turn implies that there is a negative

M. Sato (✉)
School of International and Public Policy, Hitotsubashi University, Kunitachi, Japan
e-mail: satom@econ.hit-u.ac.jp

A. Kamesaka and F. Waldenberger (eds.), *Governance, Risk and Financial Impact of Mega Disasters*, Economics, Law, and Institutions in Asia Pacific,
https://doi.org/10.1007/978-981-13-9005-0_3

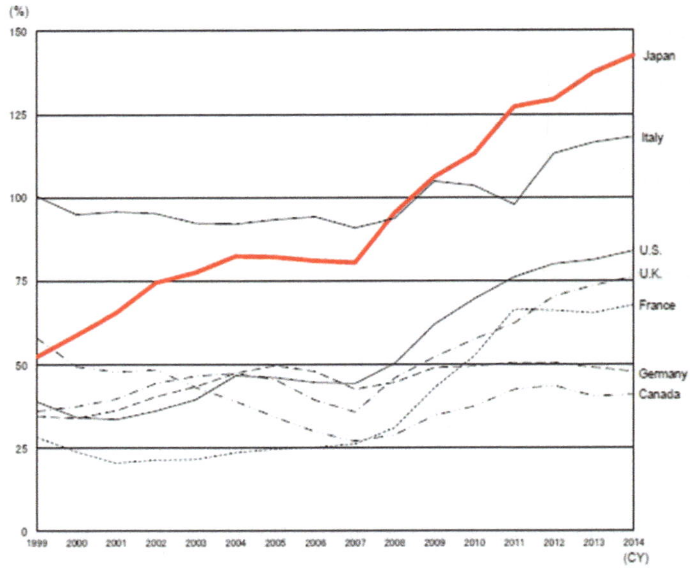

Fig. 1 International comparison of net public debt as % of GDP. *Source* Ministry of Finance (2014)

GDP gap with excess production and too little macroeconomic demand; therefore, the shock of the earthquake does not affect the macro economy too greatly. However, the story does not end here. The earthquake in Tokyo could increase the probability of the government going bankrupt because the government is urged to spend a lot of money to reconstruct the economy. This inevitably increases the public deficit substantially. The additional debt burden will turn out to be the final blow to Japan's public finance that has deteriorated in the last quarter of the century after the bursting of the bubble economy in the early 1990s. The probability of bankruptcy is lowered if fiscal consolidation efforts are put in place in advance.

Next, I will address the current situation of Japan's public finance. Figure 1 shows an international comparison of the general government net debt to GDP. For reference, the general government includes the central government, local government, as well as the social security fund. Japan is actually the worst among the major industrial economies. The net public debt ratio currently exceeds 120% of the GDP and is growing at an accelerated rate. The debt ratio is even higher than Greece. In gross terms, the debt ratio to the GDP is more than 200%. In the literature, it is known that for public finance to be sustainable, primary fiscal balance defined as tax revenue minus public spending net of debt repayment needs to be improved and turned positive to stop public debt from further accumulating. Such a trend, however, has not been observed in Japan. It is then obvious that the government's financial situation cannot be sustained. Extra-ordinary monetary easing conducted by the Bank of Japan including the net-purchases of 343 trillion yen of JGB (Japan Government

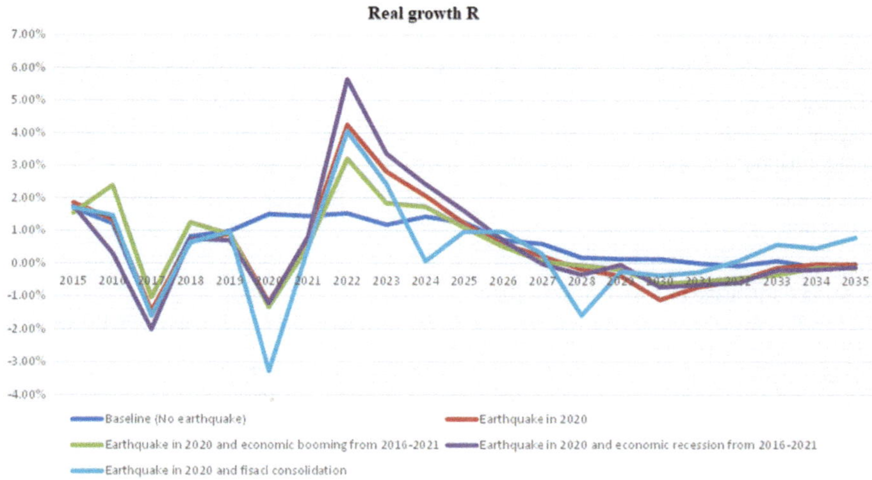

Fig. 2 Real growth R

Bonds) over the period from April 2013 to the end of 2017,[1] enabled the government to keep its interest rate at historically low levels, even in the negative. But the question remains as to how long such monetary policy can last. The central government issues more than 100 trillion yen of JGB including new and refinancing bonds. A one percentage point increase in the JGB interest rate raises interest payments by the government one trillion yen every year (Fig. 2).

One may suggest that such a debt problem will be resolved once the Japanese economy moves out of the current deflation spiral. However, the public deficit is structural rather than cyclical. The situation of public finance does not change very much even if *Abenomics* succeeds. Even if our economy recovers, we will still have a huge accumulated debt. This is because Japanese society is rapidly aging, which also leads to higher social expenditures including pensions, healthcare, and nursing care. It is projected that these social expenditures will surge in the next decades as the elderly ratio to overall population rises to as high as 40% in 2040. The government thus has a huge financial liability. To deal with the public debt problem, the government has initiated a fiscal consolidation program so as to remove the primary fiscal balance deficit by FY2020. The program contains a consumption tax increase from originally 8–10% in 2017. But the tax hike has been delayed until October 2019. The updated projection of the Cabinet Office reveals that there remains 8.3 trillion or 1.4% of GDP in primary fiscal deficit in FY2020 even in the circumstance that the Japanese economy recovers and achieves a nominal growth rate of 3%. The situation is even worse if the economy overall remains stagnant. Overall, the potential risk of government bankruptcy seems to be high at this point even without an earth-

[1]Calculated on the basis of the Bank of Japan's flow of funds statistics (http://www.boj.or.jp/en/statistics/sj/index.htm/).

Table 1 List of scenarios

	Scenario 1	Scenario 2	Scenario 3	Scenario 4	Scenario 5	Scenario 6
Earthquake		X	X	X	X	
Fiscal consolidation			X			X
Economic condition				Booming	Recession	

Notes
(i) Mega Earthquake in Tokyo: Year = 2020
(ii) Fiscal consolidation: Increasing VAT rate to 10% in April 2017 with improving PB (as % of GDP) by 2.5% respectively in 2020, 2024, 2028
(iii) Economic booming: Real growth rate +10% between 2016 and 2021
(iv) Economic stagnation: Real growth rate 1% between 2016 and 2021

quake. Given that the central government is expected to serve as the last resort and be responsible for economic recovery, a natural disaster such as a mega earthquake in Tokyo could expose the risk of Japan's public finance (Table 1).

Let me turn to the scenarios in the simulation. The simulation considers six different scenarios. In the baseline case or scenario 1, there is no earthquake and Japan's economy stays on its present course. In scenario 2, an earthquake occurs in the year 2020. Scenario 3 is the case that we have an earthquake, but the government a priori takes fiscal consolidation before the earthquake, such as increasing the VAT rate up to 10% in April 2017. Beside the tax hike, the government contains public expenditure to improve primary fiscal balance by 2.5% of GDP in 2020, 2024 and 2028. Given the actual postponement of the VAT tax increase, scenario 3 turns out to be rather hypothetical. It indicates what would happen, had the government consolidated before 2020. In scenario 6, the fiscal consolidation after 2020 takes place alongside the reconstruction spending. In this scenario, the government is serious about fiscal consolidations, although as I noted earlier, the tax hike has been delayed to 2019 in the actual scenario. There are other cases. What if we are lucky and the economy is booming before the earthquake? Scenario 4 considers the case that the growth rate is one percentage point higher than the baseline scenario between 2016 and 2021. In contrast, scenario 5 studies the economy under recession before the earthquake with real growth being lowered by one percentage point. For reference, we also examine the case that fiscal consolidation is taken but there is no earthquake.

As noted above, the model is based on a Keynesian macroeconomic model. The model is largely divided into four sectors, (1) a flow-based macro economy including consumption and investment, (2) a stock-based sector representing capital and financial assets, (3) a government sector that determines the path of the public debt stock, and (4) the sector determining the JGB interest rate and exchange rate. Without a microeconomic foundation in terms of behavioral responses of households and firms, the equations listed in the appendix are a bit ad hoc, but they still capture some economic intuition. In the sector representing the flow-based macro economy, inflation rates depend upon the GDP gap, and the exchange rate. Production is given by a Cobb-Douglas technology, which is the standard assumption for such models. Private consumption denoted by PC depends upon GDP corresponding to income in the previous period, whereas private investment is a function of JGB (market) interest rate and GDP. These are affected by variables in the previous period which introduce dynamism into the model. In the present context, macroeconomic stocks refer to private capital and private assets. Importantly, we include the government sector because we would like to account for public debt accumulation after the earthquake. We do not impose the transversality condition or the condition that the present value of public debt converges to zero as time passes. This implies that public finance may not be sustainable as addressed earlier. I also consider the JGB (Japan Government Bonds) market. The determination of the JGB interest rate is standard. The exchange rate given by e follows the interest parity condition. It includes public debt as well in order to reflect the impact of solvency risk. The coefficients of these equations are to be estimated simultaneously. To be concise, the appendix contains the variables and the equations of the macroeconomic model.

Next, I will consider projections regarding direct damage on private capital stock and on death as well as injuries. I also consider the scenario of government spending for reconstruction after the earthquake in 2020. Projections regarding direct damage, death and injuries are taken from the government estimates. The direct damage is estimated to amount to 66.6 trillion yen. Adding indirect damage such as interruption of production, the total damage to the Japanese economy reaches more than 100 trillion yen or about 20% of GDP. Regarding public spending on recovery, we adopt the data from the Hanshin-Awaji Earthquake in 1995. We calibrated government spending after the Tokyo mega earthquake using the data from the Hanshin-Awaji Earthquake (Table 2). The presumption is that the reconstruction expenditure of the former increases in proportion to direct damage, i.e. by 66.6/9.9, with 66.6 representing the expected direct damage and 9.9 the damage incurred by the Hanshin-Awaji Earthquake. The GDP and tax revenue losses are estimated likewise. We have 11 years of data regarding reconstruction spending after the Hanshin-Awaji Earthquake. The first two years are combined since the earthquake occurred in January of 1995, almost the end of FY1994 in Japan. I use the data from the Hanshin-Awaji Earthquake rather than the Great East Japan Earthquake of 2011 because the former hit a large city like Kobe with a high population density, whereas the latter affected a relatively rural area with a low population density, with the exception of the city of Sendai. Moreover, in the Great East Japan Earthquake it was the tsunami after the earthquake that caused considerable losses of lives and major damage. Taken together, the features of the Hanshin-Awaji Earthquake are closer to the projected scenario for a mega Tokyo earthquake.

The analysis takes the following steps. In Step 1, using the macroeconomic data such as consumption, GDP inflation and the JGB rate available from 1980 to 2013, I simultaneously estimate parameters of the model equations listed in the figure. The coefficients of the disturbance terms are estimated as well. The estimated values are omitted in the paper as there are too many, but all of them are statistically significant and take the expected sign. In Step 2, we introduce the shock of the earthquake to the estimated equations. For instance, labor supply decreases by 70,000 due to

Table 2 Estimation of damage and reconstruction expenditure

		Hanshin Awaji earthquake (1995)	Tokyo metropolitan earthquake
Loss of regional GDP (¥ trillion)	$DGDP_t$	2.6	39.0
Direct damage (¥ trillion)	DK_t	9.9	66.6
Tax revenue loss (¥ trillion)	DR_t	0.4	2.7
Death (ten thousands)	DL_t	0.6434	1.1
Injuries (ten thousands)		4.3792	21.0
Serious injuries (ten thousands)		1.0683	3.7
Additional expense for Reconstruction (¥Billion10)	DGI_t	Hanshin Awaji earthquake (1995)	Tokyo metropolitan earthquake
Year 1 = The earthquake year		608.24	24013.84
Year 2		2,964.07	8,157.53
Year 3		1,213.52	7,220.11
Year 4		1,074.07	5,564.67
Year 5		827.80	4,587.36
Year 6		682.42	4,308.13
Year 7		640.88	3,590.11
Year 8		534.07	2,971.81
Year 9		442.09	2,353.52
Year 10		350.11	2,253.79
Year 11		335.27	

deaths and injuries. DL in the production function Eq. (2) takes this value in 2020. In Eq. (3) DGDP in 2020 becomes 39 trillion yen. In Step 3, we generate random variables that are added to the macroeconomic equations. This is what we call a Monte Carlo simulation. Thus, both the shock due to the earthquake and the shock of some random variables are accounted for. Based on this, 5,000 simulations were conducted. The simulations are from 2015 to 2035. Structural change such as the aging of society is incorporated in the simulation. Step 4 takes the average of the macroeconomic variables such as growth and JGB rates to display the results.

Now we will turn to the results of the simulations. First, I consider the effect of the earthquake on the real growth rate. Obviously in 2020, the growth rate declines to minus 1.2% points whereas the baseline scenario records 1.5% in real terms. Decrease in the growth rate is most severe in Scenario 3 in which the fiscal consolidation including government expenditure takes place in the year of the earthquake. This may be intuitive. In all cases, however, the growth rate recovers relatively quickly. This is largely due to the government recovery spending which serves to boost macro demand. Note that the earthquake shock is a shock on production. When there is a negative GDP gap in the economy prior to the earthquake or excess supply capacity relative to demand, the damage on the supply side would not be translated into inflation, nor would it limit growth very much. It is rather the low demand that constrains the economy. The recovery spending by the government thus serves to help the macro economy in bringing about a quick recovery. This is clearly observed in Scenario 3 which assumes an economic recession from 2016 to 2021.

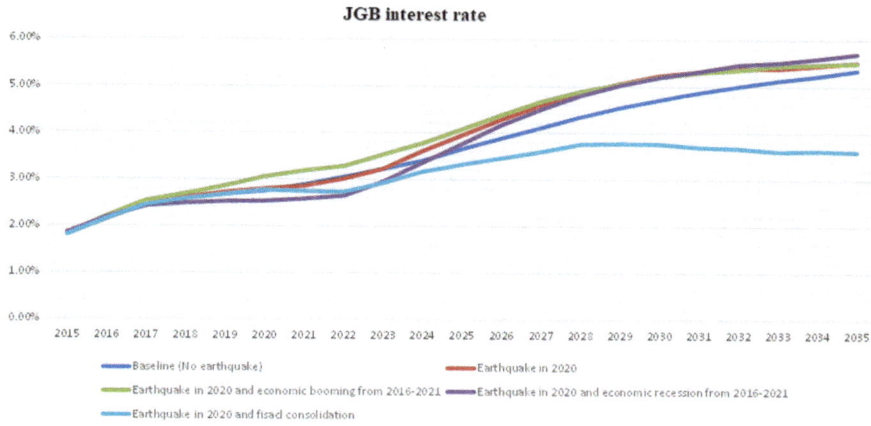

Fig. 3 JGB interest rate

In contrast, in the scenario where the earthquake occurs when the economy is booming, the recovery turns out to be slow because the economy is a bit tight. With the GDP gap being small, a surge in macro demand due to government spending leads to inflation; higher inflation generates higher interest rates which hinders growth, crowding out private investment. Interestingly, in all scenarios, the growth rate diminishes in the late 2020s, because the reconstruction spending ends, and the overall labor force decreases. Scenario 5 with fiscal consolidation reveals a different prospect of real growth in the 2030s. The growth rate in this case is higher than in the other scenarios. This is because a lower stock of outstanding government bonds allows interest rates to remain low, which works to raise investment. The simulation therefore confirms the view that fiscal consolidation promotes growth in the long run.

The following Fig. 3 shows simulation results of the JGB interest rates. As mentioned above, in the case of an earthquake in 2020 with fiscal consolidation, interest rates remain low in the long run. Otherwise, interest rates increase. The interest rates grow higher in Scenario 3 with the economic boom before the earthquake reflecting the tight macro economy. Note that even in the baseline case interest rates increase due to public debt being accumulated without fiscal consolidation.

Next, I will turn to inflation rates by focusing on the following three scenarios: the baseline case, and the cases of an earthquake with and without fiscal consolidation (Fig. 4). The good news for *Abenomics* is that eventually the economy escapes from deflation in the baseline case, but it occurs ten years later. An earthquake obviously triggers higher inflation, but it is not that high. The hyperinflation that might be expected would not occur.

The next two Figs. 5 and 6 show the path of accumulated public debt and the primary balance relative to GDP. With or without the earthquake, the public debt ratio increases over the years, exceeding 500% in 2035. If there is fiscal consolidation in place, the rate of increase will be contained. The primary fiscal balance remains in

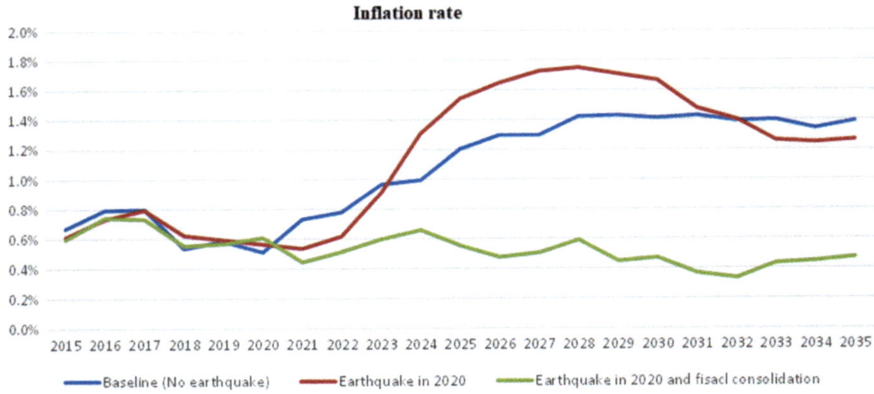

Fig. 4 Inflation rate

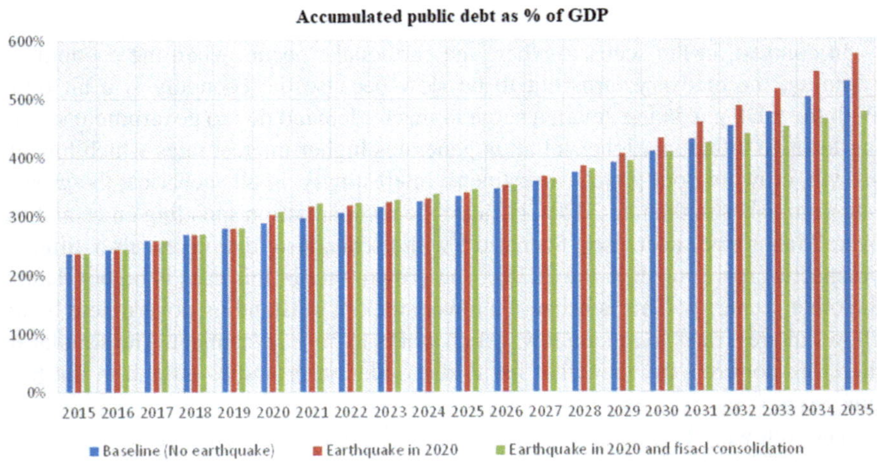

Fig. 5 Accumulated public debt as % of GDP

red in all years, i.e., adding new debt to existing stock, without fiscal consolidation. Overall it can be seen that Japan's public finance does not seem to be sustainable, with the earthquake making the public financial situation worse.

What happens to public finance? The Tokyo mega earthquake could trigger a fiscal crisis. The fiscal crisis in the present context refers to the circumstance that the government needs to refinance at higher interest rates: the JGB interest rate surges in a non-linear manner as being observed in the Greece fiscal crisis. There has been a so-called JGB paradox in which public debt has been accumulated over time while the JGB rate has declined and remained low. The paradox arises because of long-standing deflation decreasing private investment and thereby lowering demand for capital, combined with a home bias in which domestic investors managing domestic financial assets including deposit and pension funds prefer to invest in domestic sectors instead

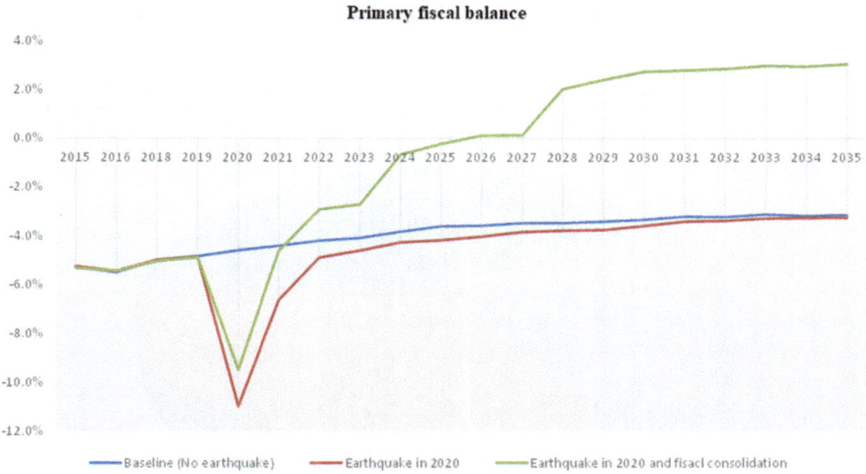

Fig. 6 Primary fiscal balance as % of GDP

of investing abroad, even if the return on foreign investment is higher. The paradox may reflect their risk averseness or a sort of inertia avoiding radical change in their portfolio holdings. This allows the government to finance their deficit in a very steady way over the years. The paradox has been reinforced in recent years with extra-ordinal monetary loosening initiated by the Bank of Japan, including the commitment to purchase 80 trillion yen of JGB annually starting in 2013. Consequently, the share of the BOJ held stock of outstanding JGB has steadily increased, whereas the share of foreign investors has remained below 10%. In 2018, the share of BOJ reached 50%. One may think that so-called helicopter money or monetization if it takes place can remove public debt, but it should be reminded that the expansion of the monetary base due to the purchases of JGB could trigger high inflation in the future. Besides expansionary monetary policy, there is also a very strong home bias among domestic asset owners. However, things will change as soon as domestic financial assets at one point are no longer able to absorb all JGB anymore. In that case, the JGB rate will surge as the government must then rely on foreign investors to finance the deficit and foreign investors place less confidence in JGB and thus rate it relatively lower than domestic investors. Here, I assume that Japan enters a fiscal crisis if the JGB share in total domestic financial assets exceeds 90%. We subtract 10% as it needs to be retained for the equity holding. The Monte Carlo simulations allow us to calculate the tendency or probability of this event to occur.

So, what is the probability of fiscal crisis? I show the probability in the years 2025, 2035, and 2040. Even without an earthquake, the Japanese government will certainly go bankrupt or be confronted with a surge in the JGB interest rate (charged by foreign investors) by 2040. If there is an earthquake, the probability of bankruptcy jumps to 40% in the year 2025 whereas in the baseline case, that percentage is only nine percent. Here, the event of a certain bankruptcy would occur in 2035. In short, over the years we will run into bankruptcy under all scenarios. So what does a mega earthquake

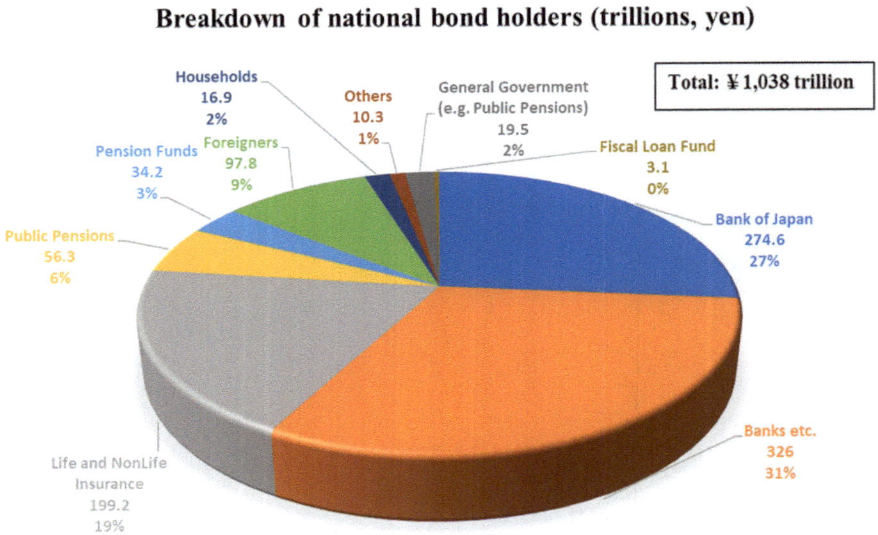

Fig. 7 Breakdown of national bond holders. *Source* Ministry of Finance (2016)

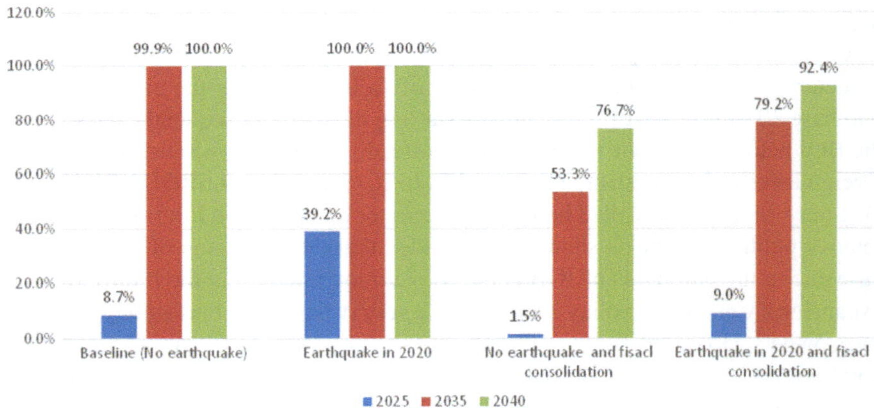

Fig. 8 Probability of fiscal crisis

do? How does the impact of the mega earthquake on public finance make fiscal crisis occur earlier? What if there is an earthquake but with fiscal consolidation? The good news is that the probability turns out to be a bit lower, relative to the case of the earthquake without fiscal consolidation. Still, we have a relatively high percentage, and a high probability of bankruptcy. That means that the fiscal consolidation of our scenario including a hike of the VAT rate to 10% and cutting public spending would have not been sufficient (Figs. 7, 8).

In summary, the impact of a mega earthquake in Tokyo is quite substantial on the macro economy in the short run, but overall, the economy will recover soon thereafter.

However, this is not because the Japanese economy is very resilient. On the contrary, the Japanese economy is very weak. Even without an earthquake, the population is declining and society is aging, and these weak conditions of the Japanese economy makes it relatively insensitive to large shocks such as a mega earthquake. A mega earthquake could have a considerable impact and could turn out to be the final blow to Japan's public finance. However, even without a mega earthquake, the JGB paradox will not continue forever and the Japanese government will go bankrupt in the sense that it will confront the difficulty of financing its deficit or be urged to pay high interest rates demanded by foreign investors as the Greek experienced during the fiscal crisis. The earthquake just makes this event occur earlier.

Appendix

See Table 3.

List of equations

$$\pi_t = c_1 + c_2(1 + GDP_{t-1} + c_3\left(\frac{e_{t-1}}{e_{t-2}} - 1\right) + \sigma_1\varepsilon_t^{\pi} \tag{1}$$

$$Y_t = A_t[RK_t]^{\alpha}[(L_t - DL_t)HL_t]^{1-\alpha} \tag{2}$$

$$\begin{aligned}\log(GDP_t) = {} & c_4 + c_5\log(PC_t) + c_6\log(PI_t) + c_7\log(GC_t + GI_t + DGI_t) \\ & + c_8NE_t - DGDP_t + \sigma_2\varepsilon_t^{GDP}\end{aligned} \tag{3}$$

$$PC_t = c_9 + c_{10}GDP_{t-1} + c_{11}GR_{t-1} + \sigma_3\varepsilon_t^{PC} \tag{4}$$

$$\log(PI_t) = c_{12} + c_{13}\log(GDP_{t-1}) + c_{14}JGBR_{t-1} + \sigma_4\varepsilon_t^{PI} \tag{5}$$

Table 3 List of variables

e_t = Exchange rate	GC_t = Government consumption	Gi_t = Government investment
GPI_t = Inflation rate	GR_t = Government tax revenue	HL_t = Labor hours
$JGBR_{t-1}$ = JGB interest rate	K_t = Capital	L_t = Labor force
NE_t = Net export	OR_t = Old age rate	PA_t = Private financial asset
PC_t = Private consumption	PD_t = public debt ratio to GDP	Pl_t = Private capital
π_t = Inflation rate	u_t = Unemployment rate	Y_t = Output (Potential GDP)

Note Variable starting with D represents earthquake shock

$$\frac{NE_t}{GDP_{t-1}} = c_{15}\frac{NE_{t-1}}{GDP_{t-2}} + c_{16}\log(e_t/GPI_t) + \sigma_5\varepsilon_t^{NE} \tag{6}$$

(2) Macro economy (Stock based)

$$K_t = c_{17}K_{t-1} + c_{18}PI_t - DK_t + \sigma_6\varepsilon_t^{K} \tag{7}$$

$$\log(PA_t) = c_{19}\log(PD_t \times GDP_t) + c_{20}\log(K_t) + \sigma_7\varepsilon_t^{PA} \tag{8}$$

(3) Government Sector

$$PB_t = GR_t - \frac{GC_t + GI_t + DGI_t}{GDP_t} + \sigma_8\varepsilon_t^{PB}$$
$$\left(GR_t \equiv \left(c_{21} + c_{22}\frac{(GDP_{t-1})^{\xi}}{GDP_t} - DR_t + DPB_t\right) \times GDP_t\right) \tag{9}$$

$$GC_t = c_{23} + c_{24}GDP_{t-1} + c_{25}OR_t + \sigma_9\varepsilon_t^{GC} \tag{10}$$

(4) JGB interest rate

$$JGBR_t = c_{26}JGBR_{t-1} + c_{27}\frac{PD_{t-1} \times GDP_{t-1}}{PA_{t-1}} + c_{28}\pi_t + \sigma_{10}\varepsilon_t^{JGBR} \tag{11}$$

$$GPI_t = c_{29}GPI_{t-1}(1 + \pi_t) + \sigma_{11}\varepsilon_t^{GPI} \tag{12}$$

$$\log(e_t) = c_{30}\log(e_{t-1}) + c_{31}\log(JGBR_t) + c_{32}(PD_{t-1}/PD_{t-2} - 1) + \sigma_{12}\varepsilon_t^{re} \tag{13}$$

$$u_t = c_{33} + c_{34}(1 + \pi_t) + \sigma_{13}\varepsilon_t^{u} \tag{14}$$

References

Ministry of Finance (2014) Japanese public finance factsheet. https://www.mof.go.jp/english/budget/budget/fy2014/factsheet2014.pdf

Ministry of Finance (2016) Japanese public finance factsheet. https://www.mof.go.jp/english/budget/budget/fy2016/03.pdf

Oguro K, Sato M (2011) Shuto chokka jishin ga makuro keizai ni oyobosu eikyô ni tsuite no bunseki (Simulation analysis of macroeconomic impact of large-scale earthquake in Tokyo). Keizai Bunseki (Economic Analysis), No 184

Chapter 4
Law and Policy Responses to Disaster-Induced Financial Distress

The Tsunami Victims of 3/11

Julius Weitzdörfer and Simon Beard

Abstract This chapter treats disaster response policies directed at the economic recovery of private households. First, we examine problems of disaster-induced financial distress from a legal and economic perspective. We do this both qualitatively and quantitatively, and focussing on residential loans, using the victims of the 11 March 2011 tsunami as our example. Then, using doctrinal and systematic analysis, we set out the broad array of law and policy solutions tackling disaster-induced debt launched by the Japanese Government. On this basis, we assess the strengths and weaknesses of these measures in terms of their practical adequacy to prevent and mitigate financial hardship and examine them against multiple dimensions of disaster justice. We conclude with suggestions for improving financial disaster recovery by taking a prospective approach, preventing the snowballing of disaster-related losses, which we argue represents a equitable and effective way forward in allocating resources following future mega disasters.

1 Japan's 2011 Tsunami and Post-disaster Debt

On 11 March 2011, the Great East Japan Earthquake, followed by a tsunami and a nuclear accident, struck the Tôhoku-region of Japan. The triple catastrophe, named *Higashi-nihon dai-shinsai,* or 3/11, unleashed the strongest tremors ever recorded in the country and waves towering up 12 m high, reaching altitudes of up to 40 m and travelling ten kilometres inland. Though many could escape in the time between the earthquake and the coming of the wave owing to sophisticated warning systems and swift evacuations, nearly 19,000 did not survive.[1]

[1]For an overview of the 3/11 disaster from the perspective of the natural sciences, see e.g. Satake (2014); from the social sciences, see e.g. Gill et al. (2013a), Kingston (2013, pp. 198–220); from socio-legal studies, see the contributions in Butt et al. (2014).

[2]See e.g. Economist (2011), see also Ranghieri and Ishiwatari (2014).

J. Weitzdörfer (✉) · S. Beard
Centre for the Study of Existential Risk, University of Cambridge, Cambridge, UK
e-mail: jfww2@cam.ac.uk

A. Kamesaka and F. Waldenberger (eds.), *Governance, Risk and Financial Impact of Mega Disasters*, Economics, Law, and Institutions in Asia Pacific,
https://doi.org/10.1007/978-981-13-9005-0_4

The earthquake made houses collapse, burn down, or fall victim to ground liquefaction and slippage. However, it did not cause the majority of damage to buildings (*tatemono songai*). More destructive was the tsunami that hit wide swaths of the rural coastline, sweeping away entire neighbourhoods, leaving more than one million buildings recorded as destroyed or damaged. Soon, the loss of electricity, due to both the tremors and the waves, caused core meltdowns and hydrogen explosions at the *Fukushima Dai'ichi* Nuclear Power Station, which added the third dimension to what had turned into a complex mega disaster. It attracted global attention and, according to the World Bank, was the world's costliest natural disaster.[2]

As 200,000 homes were lost entirely, over 300,000 people were rendered homeless, evacuated and dispersed across eight prefectures.[3] Former homeowners, shopkeepers, farmers, and fishermen found themselves penniless in shelters and evacuation centres. The evacuees (*hinan-sha*) included those who were ordered to or chose to evacuate due to the nuclear accident (*higai-sha*), a group only partly overlapping with those directly affected by the disaster's natural hazards (*hisai-sha*). Many of the latter have become the victims of another disaster, which has received much less attention: the so-called "double-loan crisis."

Broadly defined, double-loans are framed as credit to be "taken out by people or companies to rebuild their homes or other property and replace business equipment—while still having to repay loans taken out before the disasters." (Japan Times 2013). Double-loan problems (*nijû rôn mondai*) are, therefore, post-disaster problems of over-indebtedness and access-to-credit, rooted in pre-disaster obligations that were disaster-prone yet uninsured or underinsured. They occur in scenarios where mortgaged homes are destroyed or declared uninhabitable, where vehicles, vessels, machinery and other commodities bought on credit were swept away, and where whole factories, serving as collateral for corporate debt, vanished in the waves.[4] Dispossessed, often jobless and traumatised, victims find themselves in the desperate position of seeking new loans to restart their lives, while being unable to meet their previous obligations or offer any security. Companies that have made capital investments and are willing to restore their productive assets are facing similar issues and, eventually, bankruptcy. In the aftermath of 3/11, tsunami victims facing double-loans became a vulnerable group "unable to rebuild their lives through their own efforts."[5]

As we will show, the tsunami carried a systemic risk in that it triggered cascading financial disruptions endangering economic and social systems: Double-loans harm disaster victims, delay reconstruction, and accelerate depopulation. They play a major role in disaster-induced defaults, denial of new credit, insolvency, and foreclosure, promoting various forms of homelessness as well as long-term, long-distance displacement. Regional financial institutions and creditors were themselves direct or

---

[3]Three days into the catastrophe, the number of displaced had peaked at almost half a million people. Out of this group, 300,000 evacuees remained in temporary housing well into 2013, of which less than 100,000 remained in 2016, see Kozuka (2012, p. 4), Japan Times (2012, 2013), Ueda and Shaw (2014, pp. 210–211).

[4]See e.g. Dôjima hôritsu jimu-sho [Dôjima Law Office] (2011, p. 126).

[5]See also Cho (2014, p. 171).

indirect victims of the disaster and overwhelmed by the situation.[6] Thus, many were hardly in an economic position to grant infinite debt freezes or interest concessions to affected individuals and corporations, let alone benevolent and generous acquittals of debt. Voluntary write-offs would have been legally questionable considering the banks' fiduciary duties to their shareholders and depositors. Lowering the credit standards for disaster-affected borrowers could have been an option, but would have required government support by guarantees or allowing high interest rates to offset the increased risk of default. Due to the absence of sufficient private insurance and public compensation, double-loan problems have come to be regarded as entrenching social inequality, constituting a significant threat to regional financial institutions, and posing considerable obstacles to overall disaster recovery, for which even the Japanese Prime Minister acknowledged an urgent "need for some creative ideas."[7]

Despite its seriousness and an abundance of Japanese scholarship and media coverage, this pressing issue has been little investigated in scholarly writing.[8] Not only the wide range of law and policy measures deployed, but also the complexities of addressing the crisis in a socially just, yet feasible manner, remain unexamined. Therefore, we investigate this case to help tackle future disaster-related indebtedness and home-less-ness in high-risk locations.[9] This is equally important in developed countries with high home-ownership rates, such as the USA with regard to recurring hurricanes, as well as in developing countries, such as in South Asia, where micro-credit is in use. The problems are interdisciplinary in nature, falling between law, economics, moral philosophy, sociology, and disaster studies, as well as the planning, building and housing literature. We therefor seek to address these problems by drawing on all these fields.

As a study of disaster response directed at the financial recovery of private households, this chapter complements the chapters in this edited volume that cover the fiscal dimensions of disaster risk financing. In the next section, Sect. 2, we will introduce the difficult situation of double-loan victims from a social and economic perspective. We will attempt to do this qualitatively and quantitatively, and focussing on residential loans. In Sect. 3, we will set out, via doctrinal and systematic analysis, the broad array of law and policy solutions tackling disaster-induced debt and homelessness launched by governmental and non-governmental actors. On this basis,

---

[6]See Steele and Jin (2012, pp. 47–48).

[7]Prime Minister Naoto Kan, as cited by Shozaburo Jimi, Minister of Financial Services, see Financial Services Agency (2011b).

[8]Indeed, some Japanese commentators point out that the issue has not been fully grasped even in Japan. For the few brief mentions in western languages, see Kabashima (2012, pp. 13–15); otherwise only Wakabayashi et al. (2011) (two paragraphs); Umeda (2013, pp. 18–19) (one paragraph); Cho (2014, p. 171) (one paragraph); and a box in Ranghieri and Ishiwatari (2014, pp. 274–275). Through the lens of insolvency law, guidelines stipulated for out-of-court settlements with double-loan victims have been analysed in detail by Steele and Jin (2012). For a first overview in Japanese, see Adachi (2011). However, these procedures constitute merely one of the regulatory responses, unfortunately unsuccessful in practice, leaving the crisis largely unresolved.

[9]Elsewhere, we examine the related problems of homelessness, the provision of housing, and the resulting questions of disaster justice in greater detail: Weitzdörfer and Beard (forthcoming 2020).

Sect. 4 begins by assessing the strengths and weak-nesses of the counter-measures in terms of their practical adequacy to prevent and mitigate financial hardship. We then examine disaster debt against multiple dimensions of social justice. Finally, we conclude by making several suggestions for improving disaster recovery. We argue that taking a prospective approach based on preventing the snowballing of disaster damages hampering reconstruction and recovery represents a better way forward in allocating resources following future mega disasters.

2 Double-Loans as a Key Challenge for Financial Recovery

Although forms of post-disaster indebtedness constitute a phenomenon observable world-wide and residential property-ownership is a crucial substitute for social security not only in Japan,[10] certain aggravating factors make the case at hand unique. This is not only due to the unprecedented amount of damage done by the 3/11 tsunami. It is also due to the exceptional scarcity of inhabitable land in mountainous Japan and a general lack of homes (*jûtaku busoku*), increased by new building restrictions in the ravaged areas, and paired with some of the world's highest real estate prices.[11] The mortgage market, with a volume of around JPY 180 billion, is crucial to Japan's financial economy and was widely regarded as threatened by a domino effect from the institutions, some of whose "operational bases were almost entirely destroyed by the disaster." (Ranghieri and Ishiwatari 2014, p. 275).

As a basic fact, rebuilding requires financing, and as such is often shied away from by victims already in debt (Ohira and Chiba 2011). According to estimations by the Financial Services Agency (*Kin'yû-chô*, FSA), "disaster-hit firms and individuals have around $7.2 billion in loans outstanding." (Wakabayashi et al. 2011). As a result, many of those affected are reportedly "forced to relinquish self-help rebuilding projects because of 'double-loan' problems." (Cho 2014, p. 171). This also constitutes a difficult issue in the process of moving back to permanent housing in line with community relocation plans (Kitamura 2011, p. 57; Kabashima 2012, p. 13), increasing the challenge for local authorities to provide affordable residences[12] and contributing to the outflow of population.[13] In other words, "the crushing burden of debts, along with damage from the quake, (…) result in a vicious circle that will further exhaust affected areas." (Katô 2013).

In Japanese, both the terms "double-loan" (*nijû rôn*; *daburu rôn*) and "double-debt" (*nijû saimu*) are in use, distinguishing the phenomenon from common forms of

[10]On Japan, see Hirayama and Hayakawa (1995, p. 230), Hirayama (2010); similar problems occurred, for example, in New Orleans in the wake of Hurricane Katrina, although not referred to with a special term.

[11]While a new home is said to cost the equivalent of three years' salary in the USA, the figure is five to eight years in Japan; see also generally Hirayama and Hayakawa (1995, p. 215).

[12]See generally Gill et al. (2013b, pp. 9–11), Godzik (2013), Ueda and Shaw (2014).

[13]See e.g. Cho (2014, p. 170).

personal over-indebtedness (*tajû saimu mondai*), a widespread issue in post-bubble Japan. Further to the broad definition above, it must be noted that, in many cases, a second (i.e. double) loan is not even available, when indebted victims are rejected outright by financial institutions. It follows that the double-loan problem is twofold, with some disaster victims facing double-indebtedness and others denied access to credit. Moreover, new loans are rarely equivalent to the previous outstanding loans,[14] as the adjective "double" might suggest.

As introduced above, double-loans both affected debt positions of private household and of businesses, but the Government only directly alleviated the latter by measures of debt factoring. Therefore, what remained at the heart of the crisis was the ruinous loss of home-ownership, "which, against a background of continually rising land prices and inadequacies in the country's social-security system, [had] taken on the character of wealth formation and a substitute for social security." (Hirayama and Hayakawa 1995, p. 230).[15] Here, collateralised debt in tsunami-prone areas constituted a specific kind of pre-disaster vulnerability of physical assets, crystallising into social vulnerabilities of homelessness and over-indebtedness for borrowers, as well as economic loss in terms of credit defaults for lenders.

Accordingly, Japanese politicians and scholars agreed that "an adequate measure against this issue is necessary for reviving the economic and social life (…) economic revival and city reconstruction." (Kabashima 2012, pp. 8–13).[16] Equally, the Japan Federation of Bar Associations (*nichiben-ren*, JFBA), representing the country's licensed attorneys, expressed increasing concerns that "the loan problem not only forces disaster victims to restart in the red, it is also a serious problem influencing the business of regional financial institutions." (JFBA 2011a, p. 63).[17] It can therefore be concluded that, two decades after the bad-loan problems of the burst bubble, the collapse of the *jûsen* mortgage lending companies, the economic shock of 3/11, and in addition to ever-growing sovereign debt, double-loans present yet another kind of domestic crisis for Japan.

The practical relevance of double-loan problems is evidenced by data gathered in consultations with victims in the aftermath of 3/11.[18] National disaster-counselling (*Shinsai hôterasu dayaru*) was initiated by means of the Act Concerning Special Legal Aid by the Japan Legal Support Center to assist Victims of the Great East Japan Earthquake (Law No. 6/2011),[19] designed "to help solve the legal trouble stemming from the earthquake, such as double loans." (Government of Japan, Cabinet Office 2012, Chap. 3, Sects. 7–8). As disaster victims were evacuated to sites

[14]See e.g. Ranghieri and Ishiwatari (2014, p. 274), JFBA (2011c).

[15]See also Hirayama (2010).

[16]See also Japan Press Weekly (2011b), Wakabayashi et al. (2011).

[17]See also the detailed qualitative and quantitative analyses of the resulting problems and solutions for regional financial institutions by Torihata (2012, pp. 201–207), Uchida et al. (2012), using company- and bank-level micro-data.

[18]E.g. Leflar et al. (2012, p. 77), where double-loans are listed as two out of nine major concerns.

[19]*Higashi-nihon dai-shinsai no hisai-sha ni tai suru enjo no tame no nihon shihô shi'en sentâ no gyômu no tokurei ni kan suru hôritsu.*

all over the country, they sought advice in various ways, e.g. through the NCAC's multiple debt counselling service (*Tajû saimu sôdan madoguchi*), at the centres of the Japan Credit Counselling Organisation (*Nihon kurejitto kaunseringu kyôkai*), and even at the Money Lending Industry Counselling and Dispute Resolution Centre (*Kashikin-gyô sôdan funsô kaiketsu sentâ*).[20] Statistics compiled from the subject matter of 17,300 pro bono consultations with lawyers in onsite evacuation centres and through free telephone helplines by the JFBA (*denwa hôritsu sôdan*) demonstrate that among 24 identified legal concerns of disaster-victims, "the prevalence of consultations related to home loans, etc., is a common feature in all three disaster-affected prefectures of the Tôhoku region." (JFBA 2011a, p. 59). This applies to Iwate Prefecture in particular, where the proportion of persons with lost homes was reported as high, and where one in five persons seeking advice inquired about residential and other loans. Specifically, the association contends that, according to the surveys, "double-loan problems have been the second most important topic of consultation in evacuation centres in Miyagi Prefecture, where 65% of debtors suffer from residential mortgages exceeding JPY ten million, and among the top five in the other prefectures." (JFBA 2011a, p. 63).[21] In absolute numbers, consultations on loans were highest in Miyagi Prefecture, with over 550 consultations in April 2011 alone (JFBA 2011a, 59–61). In summary however, the over 2000 individual loan-related consultations reported in total between March and June of 2011 fail to show the full scale of loan-related problems.[22]

Possibly due to a lack of time and money, or due to the lack of legal practitioners, thousands of debtors reportedly entered negotiations with their financial institutions directly.[23] Citibank Japan, for instance, established special procedures and a toll free telephone line for customers in disaster areas, including a housing loan counter, and offered cash withdrawals and free replacements where cash cards or the traditional personal seals (*hanko*) were lost, as long as some kind of identification could be provided (Citibank Japan 2011). Consultations regarding mortgages were widely welcomed by banks. As the Minister of Finance noted, life-insurance companies were similarly proactive and flexible with their customers.[24] Within two months, eight regional banks in the three disaster-hit Tôhoku prefectures were reported to have granted over 10,000 loan deferments to illiquid disaster victims, amounting to several hundred billion yen (Ohira and Chiba 2011). The number of loans outstanding was expected to grow once fisheries and agricultural cooperatives would be added—most affecting regional banks (Ohira and Chiba 2011).

---

[20]See also Financial Services Agency (2011d).

[21]For evidence of thousands of consultations on loans in Iwate Prefecture, see also Fig. 5 in Okamoto (2012, p. 58).

[22]This is not only due to their limited time-frame, as specific inquiries about public benefits and relief for home-owners may have been attributed to the share of consultations on "laws and regulations." In addition, a large proportion of the cases is likely not among those surveyed by the JFBA.

[23]See Ohira and Chiba (2011).

[24]See Kozuka (2012, pp. 7–8), Financial Services Agency (2011b).

As a result, the diversity of double-loan scenarios makes calculating the number of affected victims anything but easy: Over 300,000 people remained evacuees by the end of 2012, of whom, nearly one in five sought advice on loans according to the surveys cited above.[25] Out of these, "20,000 individuals [are calculated to be so highly indebted that they] are at risk of bankruptcy" according to the Wall Street Journal.[26] With regards to defaulting home loans, an estimated 8,000 to 10,000 estates concentrated in the tsunami-stricken coastal strips are said to have defaulted on loans (Japan Times 2012, 2013), affecting up to 30,000 people.[27] This implies a population of "latent homeless" and "hidden homeless" (Okamoto and Bretherton 2012)[28] in temporary accommodation, without the financial means of moving onwards, which is greater than Japan's official total number of homeless people prior to the disaster.[29]

Another manifestation of the double loans crisis is that, according to media reports, Japan's notorious consumer finance companies (*sarakin*) and unregistered black-market moneylenders (*yami-kin'yû*) have been actively taking advantage of disaster victims unable to obtain further loans from legal financial institutions.[30] This has further increased the financial burden of these victims, as evidenced by surveys of debtors (Dôshita 2012, p. 4), and there has been a surge of complaints to the National Consumer Affairs Centre (*Kokumin seikatsu sentâ*, NCAC). By June 2011, large-scale black-market unsecured money lending had become apparent in the disaster zone, at usurious interest rates exceeding the statutory cap of 15–20%, Article 1 para 1 Interest Limitation Act (Law No. 100/1954),[31] punishable with imprisonment under Article 5 Capital Subscription Act (Law No. 195/1954)[32] and under various provisions of the Money Lending Business Act (Law No. 32/1983).[33]

As high-interest loans of this kind are illegal in Japan they are more dangerous, traditionally involving strong-arm debt-collection and often conducted by organised crime groups (*bôryoku-dan*) or persons related to them. Well into 2012, there were reports of loan sharks misleading disaster victims by disguising their activities as disaster relief in Iwate Prefecture, while others targeted financially struggling small

[25]Though most elderly Japanese have high savings, according to national statistics of the same year, 53.5% of workers' households were in debt, see Ministry of Internal Affairs and Communications, Statistics Bureau (2013, p. 149). Hence, the number of evacuees suffering from pre-disaster debt may have been as high as 100,000.

[26]This is an unsourced estimation cited from Wakabayashi et al. (2011).

[27]As these rural homes likely house more than the national average of 2.5 people, Ministry of Internal Affairs and Communications, Statistics Bureau (2013, p. 13).

[28]Implying a functional definition relying on a more literal and thus wider definition of "homelessness" than the one used by the Government.

[29]Okamoto and Bretherton (2012) cite government figures suggesting that in Japan's major cities, 16,000 people "sleep rough." For a different number of 25,000 and various categories of homelessness, see Iwata (2007, pp. 142–144); more broadly on the ways of social exclusion of the poor in contemporary Japan, see Iwata and Nishizawa (2008).

[30]See e.g. Mainichi Daily News (2011).

[31]*Risoku seigen-hô.*

[32]*Shusshi no ukeire, azukari-kin oyobi kinri-tô no torishimari ni kansuru hôritsu.*

[33]*Kashikin-gyô-hô.*

and medium enterprises (SMEs) with usurious lending practices commonly known as *shôkô rôn*.[34] Worsening the situation, some victims "erroneously use their insurance coverage or relief money to repay debts or take out new loans," (Japan Times 2012)[35] even though claims for excessive interest may be deemed void under the laws outlined above.

Post-disaster inequalities, widening social disparities and polarisation due to debt and homelessness are recurring phenomena.[36] Elderly victims, often referred to as the most numerous vulnerable social group in Japan, find themselves in the least fortunate position. This is due to both their reluctance to take financial risks in the absence of successors to their businesses (Wilhelm and Delaney 2013, p. 114, p. 122) and the reluctance of credit institutions to advance further credit in light of their age (Cho 2014, p. 171).[37]

While public and political attention faded, victims' hopelessness lasted, and with regard to recovery, "gaps between economic indices and victims' actual situations" become apparent (Cho 2014, p. 171). To this day, double-loan issues continue (Cho 2014, p. 171) and still "hinder the rebuilding of people's lives and businesses in the northeast." (Japan Times 2012, 2013). Next, we explore whether this was in spite or rather because of the government's responses.

3 Financial Law and Policy Responses

The Great East Japan Disaster confronted Japan, a country under a firmly-established rule of law, with the need to resolve numerous legal issues.[38] Surveys with 3/11 victims by legal professionals suggest that 40% of those affected encountered disaster-related legal problems within 18 months (Nihon shihô shi'en senta hôterasu 2013, p. 5),[39] and disaster laws and regulations are a particularly important practical concern for victims (JFBA 2011a, p. 60; Leflar et al. 2012). Already before the disaster struck, the country had at least 52 pieces of national legislation in place solely for managing natural disasters,[40] likely constituting the world's most detailed national disaster law. Within the first three months following the disaster, an additional 20 relevant bills (*hô'an*) were introduced, and 39 cabinet orders (*seirei*) were passed by

[34] See Dôshita (2012, p. 5). Inter alia, such activities may constitute violations of Article 16 para 2 Nos. 2, 4 of the Money Lending Business Act, which ban solicitations that target persons lacking repayment capacity and that induce recipients of public benefits to borrow.

[35] See also Mainichi Daily News (2011).

[36] See Hirayama (2000, pp. 117–118), Johnson (2007, p. 445).

[37] For examples, see Wakabayashi et al. (2011).

[38] On the Government's legislative, organisational, administrative, and fiscal responses, see generally Inaba (2011); and in English, Umeda (2013).

[39] Based on interviews at home, with 1,598 out of 1,650 responding. The rate of disaster victims encountering legal problems went up by 14% in comparison with 2008.

[40] See the timeline and list in Government of Japan, Cabinet Office (2011a, pp. 4–7).

the Central Government (*chûô seifu*) alone.[41] All this was done while simultaneously dealing with specific issues related to the nuclear crisis at the *Fukushima Dai'ichi* Nuclear Power Station, compensation for victims of which, legally understood as the "largest civil liability case in … history," (Weitzdörfer 2014)[42] follows special rules of nuclear tort law and thus falls beyond the scope of this chapter.

Although double-loans are problems in debtor-creditor relationships, both governmental and non-governmental actors had soon noted[43] the scope of the challenges relating to housing, asset replacement and financial recovery regarding indebted and homeless tsunami victims. As only few of the government's measures of disaster response and recovery were exclusively directed at double-loan victims, in the following subsections, we will summarise how the government responded, directly or indirectly, to financially support disaster victims facing double-loans across the areas of disaster management, real property-, debtor-creditor- and insolvency-law, banking regulation, state aid, social welfare, and charity.[44]

3.1 Loan Deferments and Debt Factoring

Explicitly to mitigate double-loan problems, loans taken out by individuals as well as companies and stores in roughly equal proportions, were deferred, i.e. voluntarily and virtually unconditionally put under a state of forbearance, and repayment deadlines were rescheduled and postponed upon borrowers' requests after the FSA and the Governor of the Bank of Japan had called on lenders accordingly (Ohira and Chiba 2011; Financial Services Agency 2011b).[45] By extending the (post-Lehman) Act Concerning Temporary Measures to Facilitate Financing for SMEs, etc. (Law No. 96/2009),[46] the government created incentives for financial institutions by enhancing its credit guarantee system, also covering home-loans. Institutions were reported to have complied upon receiving a mere telephone call by borrowers, also refraining from charging default interest (Ohira and Chiba 2011).[47] To be fair, it has to be noted that Japan's regional banks had been offering very attractive interest rates to debtors

[41] See Inaba (2011, p. 25) for numerous examples and further references.

[42] See also Feldman (2013), Kawamura (2017).

[43] Dôjima hôritsu jimu-sho [Dôjima Law Office] (2011, p. 128).

[44] This overview is not exhaustive; see Weitzdörfer and Beard (forthcoming 2018) for more detail.

[45] See also Dôjima hôritsu jimu-sho [Dôjima Law Office] (2011, pp. 116–119).

[46] It has now expired.

[47] Such penalties are significant, as they may be as high as 40% of the principal, or twice the maximum annual interest, Article 4 para 1 of the Interest Limitation Act. Institutions might have similarly waived contractual rights to demand immediate repair of damaged real property from mortgagees.

already in the first place.[48] But loan deferments help with old loans rather than with new loans and had limited potential to solve double-loan problems.

Following public demands and political mobilisation for relief to companies affected by disaster-debt (*hisai saimu no kaihô*) by the Japanese Bar (JFBA 2011a, p. 64, d, p. 11), a regulatory package on double-loans for indebted companies was proposed by Ministers of the ruling Democratic Party of Japan (DPJ), backed even by the Communist Party (JCP) (Japan Press Weekly 2011b), establishing organisations for corporate debt factoring.[49] These public entities set up a second supplementary budget (*Sangyô fukkô kikô*) in five affected prefectures, which was approved on 25 July 2011. They were funded by local financial institutions and the prefectures (*todô fuken*) (Japan Times 2011) and offer partial or full waivers on pre-disaster obligations, yet exclusively for corporate, not personal, debts. Furthermore, such wavers are only available if the creditor is a financial institution or leasing corporation.[50] As a part of this first regulatory package, the government also asked the Japan Housing Finance Agency (*Jûtaku kin'yû shi'en kikô*) to waive mortgage repayments and to reduce its interest rates.

Astonishingly, a second system was started in March 2012, backed mainly by opposing MPs of the conservative "Liberal Democratic Party of Japan" (LDP)[51] and the FSA by means of the Double Loan Relief Act (Law No. 113/2011).[52] Under the new law, a private corporation was established,[53] now competing with the public entities in winning clients and recruiting personnel (Japan Times 2013). Under this scheme, debtor companies are expected to repay reduced sums to the support organisation after it has purchased the outstanding loan claims against them.[54]

Since the easier corporate debt cases had already been dealt with, this politically-induced rivalry caused inefficiency, and rendered municipalities and banks "caught between requests from both sides to introduce new clients." (Japan Times 2013). As a result, debt purchases were "not advancing smoothly" and affected companies were unable to secure adequate funds for recovery.[55] The redundancies created, e.g.

---

48 Serving predominantly local corporations, individuals, and public sector bodies, these 41 institutions offered long-term actual interest rates as low as 2.5 and 2.0% on average in 2011 and 2012. The Shinkin banks, a total of 270 co-operative regional financial institutions, primarily serving SMEs and local residents, operated at similarly moderate rates of 2.8 and 2.4%, respectively, see OECD (2013).

49 See also Ohira and Chiba (2011), Ranghieri and Ishiwatari (2014, p. 275).

50 See also Dôjima hôritsu jimu-sho [Dôjima Law Office] (2011, pp. 127–128).

51 To those unfamiliar with politics in Japan, it should be remarked that the LDP's name is potentially misleading, as it is neither very liberal (rather interventionist and conservative), nor democratic to the bone (rather relying on top-down decisions), nor a "party" in the European sense (rather its factions compete for power within). On differences in the crisis-management by the DPJ and the LDP, see generally Krauss (2013).

52 *Nijû rôn kyûsai-hô* or *Higashi-nihon dai-shinsai jigyô-sha saisei shi'en kikô-hô*; see Claremont (2014, p. 86, p. 96) on how political tensions in the National Diet impeded relief efforts.

53 For a comparison, see e.g. JFBA (2012a, p. 31).

54 See also Kabashima (2012, p. 13).

55 See Ando et al. (2013, p. 9).

with different consultation centres and procedures, dampened reconstruction efforts, resulting in fierce criticism and calls for integration into a single entity (Japan Times 2013). However, and in contradiction to other comments,[56] even if these schemes had succeeded, they would still have excluded important classes of disaster-affected debtors, such as home owners, and only helped SMEs (and thus their banks).[57]

3.2 Private Liquidations

Perhaps the most promising strategy forged for personal debtors was the stipulation of the Guidelines for Individual Debtor Private Liquidation (Kojin saimu-sha no shiteki seiri ni kan suru gaidorain kenkyû-kai 2011),[58] creating a system of debt workouts referred to as allegedly "the first of its kind in Japan and (…) unprecedented even in the world." (Ranghieri and Ishiwatari 2014, p. 275). The guidelines constitute a procedural remedy put underway by legal practitioners and financial institutions: Under the auspices of the FSA and the Japanese Bankers Association, and again as a consequence of the JFBA's swift and continuous mobilisation for a system of voluntary liquidations, non-judicial guidelines for private debt reorganisations (*saimu seiri*) were put in force in August 2011. The idea behind them was to avoid further bankruptcies,[59] also of individual entrepreneurs, beyond the 644 of such cases recorded in the first year alone (Katô 2013). In this way, the guidelines serve as a complement to the ordinary proceedings of bankruptcy (*hasan*) and civil rehabilitation (*minji saisei*),[60] from which they had been derived.

Accordingly, banks were expected to "partly or entirely give up their claims on housing and automobile loans if borrowers in disaster areas work out appropriate payment plans." (Japan Times 2013). For this, a so-called "Steering committee for the guidelines for individual debtor out-of-court workouts" and registered experts mediate between debtors and financial institutions to draw up a repayment plan upon debtor's request and creditor's consent.[61] The speed and flexibility (Katô 2013), the fact that such arrangements would not be recorded in debtors' credit histories (*shin'yô jôhô*), and the principle of the exclusion of guarantors' debts were repeatedly praised as merits of the guidelines (JFBA 2011a, p. 64, b, d, p. 11, 2012a, p. 28). In addition, the rather hefty regular scale of legal fees is not applied, debtors may retain a cash allowance of JPY 5 million (over five times higher than in cases of insolvency),

[56]See e.g. Ranghieri and Ishiwatari (2014, p. 275).

[57]For critical remarks, see Part 3.6(c).

[58]For a detailed description and a translation, see Steele and Jin (2012); in Japanese, see Adachi (2011).

[59]For practical advice, see Dôjima hôritsu jimu-sho [Dôjima Law Office] (2011, pp. 115–142).

[60]For their role in relation to the disaster, see generally Dôjima hôritsu jimu-sho [Dôjima Law Office] (2011, pp. 143–185), Katô (2013).

[61]See also Kabashima (2012, pp. 14–15).

charity donations are exempt from seizure, and interest payments on loans may be subsidised by the prefectures under certain conditions.[62]

Nevertheless, problems were soon identified in relation to the "user-friendliness" of the guidelines, such as the possibility of proceedings near the debtor's residence (JFBA 2011a, p. 64, d, p. 11) and a continuing lack of publicity. The procedure under the guidelines has also been criticised as overwhelmingly complicated and often misunderstood, resulting in victims having difficulty being approved as eligible (Japan Times 2012, 2013; Cho 2014, p. 171). Not surprising to many, public explanatory "seminars in rural areas attract few participants, apparently due to concerns about looking bad," and thus less shameful, direct contact with debtors was demanded.[63] The guidelines have also been criticised for their ambiguity about whether debtors can be entirely exempt from their debt, in that they were designed with the purpose of preventing bankruptcies, instead of permanently releasing debtors from their debts (Kabashima 2012, p. 14).[64] As a consequence, one panel involved has been accused "of improperly forcing bailout applicants to promise to repay a portion of their loans" and subsequently refusing to allow lawyers to supervise and screen panel meetings on bailout applications (Japan Times 2013), raising concerns of partiality and opacity.

In response, advertisements have been placed in the media, the FSA has issued a communication to financial institutions (JFBA 2012a, p. 28) and calls for amendments have been addressed by means of partial revisions. Despite this, and again contradictorily to more favourable comments in academic scholarship,[65] the carefully-drafted guidelines are far from a success—as the association itself admits.[66] Financial institutions often simply seem unwilling to concede more than a mere rescheduled repayment (*hensai no risukejyûru*) to debtors.[67]

This regrettable situation is reflected in the number of cases officially filed for debt workouts, which, despite some momentum by relocations and mortgage cancellations in 2013, still total only 1,351 as of 17 March 2017 (Kojin-ban shiteki seiri gaidorain un'ei i'in-kai 2014),[68] a figure that is dwarfed by the banks' estimations of a potential demand "close to 5,000 to 6,000" and the 200,000 homes lost (Japan Times 2012). More importantly, the relatively high count of inquiries, well above 8,000, suggests a significant unmet demand from victims.

[62]See also Kabashima (2012, p. 14).

[63]See Japan Times (2013).

[64]See also Adachi (2011, p. 9).

[65]See Steele and Jin (2012, p. 44, pp. 66–68), Katô (2013).

[66]See e.g. JFBA (2012b) (updated regularly).

[67]See JFBA (2012a, p. 28).

[68]The prefectural figures mirror Miyagi as the most affected prefecture, with two thirds of the filings, followed by Iwate with one fourth. Cho (2014, p. 171) is apparently confusing the number of applications with mere inquiries.

3.3 Consumer Credit

A vicious circle of excessive borrowing had long been understood as a major cause of so-called "multiple debt problems" (*tajû saimu mondai*) of consumers in Japan since the 1970s and had been addressed by lowering interest rate ceilings, introducing credit checks, a total amount control, and supervisory credit record institutes by a major reform that had only come into force in 2010.[69] Although restricting access to credit, these safeguards had been effective against grey-market predatory lending, well-known across Japan by company names such as *Aiful*, *Acom*, and *Promise*, and had put most of the loan sharks, already referred to above, out of business (Flynn and Taniguchi 2010).

Less than three weeks after the catastrophe, however, politicians of the DPJ took unexpected action to revive these consumer finance companies—in an effort to provide means of financial relief to disaster victims. Doing away with concerns about the integrity of this sector and the impact of interest as high as 20% annually on the financial situation of already hopelessly indebted victims, the DPJ demanded to allow further lending previously deemed illegal. Even the Bar asked the government to establish a framework that enables indebted, disaster-affected households to take out additional loans.[70]

The FSA was receptive to this and lifted restrictions by amending the relevant Cabinet Ordinance, which partly, but effectively, invalidated provisions of consumer protection, deemed a key element of the previous reform (Ordinance No. 40/1983).[71] By easing conditions stipulating, inter alia, a so-called duty of responsible lending (*sôryô kisei*), lenders were again allowed to advance loans beyond amounts borrowers would reasonably be able to repay given their annual income (*hensai nôryoku*) without renewed borrowing.[72] Furthermore, apparently by way of administrative guidance (*gyôsei-shidô*), the government called on "the public and private sectors to provide consultation services for disaster victims, subsidise loan interest for disaster-hit businesses and offer credit guarantees for firms."[73] Despite the political controversy and renewed criticism by NPOs, the FSA's "sudden deregulation" even bypassed the usual procedure of inviting public comment (*iken kôbo tetsuzuki*), Article 39 para 4 No. 1 of the Administrative Procedure Act (Law No. 88/1993).[74]

---

[69] Accordingly, Article 13 et seq. of the Money Lending Business Act imposed a duty on lenders to assess the financial situation of prospective borrowers, banned loans leading to indebtedness disproportionate in relation to the borrower's income, and imposed fines and up to one year of imprisonment upon violation in Article 48 et seq. of the act, see e.g. Kozuka and Nottage (2007) and Weitzdörfer (forthcoming).

[70] See Ohura and Chiba (2011), Japan Press Weekly (2011a).

[71] *Kashikin gyôhô shikkô kisoku*, as amended by Cabinet Ordinance No. 35/2011; Mainichi Daily News (2011); on the earlier laws, see Shimizu (2007, pp. 189–220).

[72] For a summary of the amendments, see Financial Services Agency (2011a).

[73] See Japan Times (2011).

[74] *Gyôsei tetsuzuki-hô*; the quotation is from Japan Press Weekly (2011a).

In spite of the allegedly good intentions to remove "inconveniences in borrowing" in the disaster area (Financial Services Agency 2011a) and considering the financial sector's strong backing, it remains doubtful whether the liberalisation actually was implemented to help victims of double-loans, as financing real estate and vehicles had already been exempt from credit checks from the outset, Article 12-2 Money Lending Business Act. At least the speed of deregulating consumer finance was remarkable, as not even charity money had been distributed to most victims at the time.

3.4 Charity Money

Although privately raised, charity money was also subject to government intervention—by way of selective distribution to victims. Donations to the Japan Red Cross and other charities all over the world (*gi'en-kin*), already exceeding JPY 250 billion as of May 2011 (Government of Japan, Cabinet Office 2011b, p. 7), started to be distributed by municipalities seven weeks after the catastrophe.[75]

These initial payments to affected households generally amounted to a lump sum of JPY 350,000 in cash (Brasor and Tsubuku 2011; Feldman 2013, p. 338) for any family member found dead or declared missing and deemed deceased (pursuant to Article 30 of the Civil Code; Articles 86, 89 of the Family Registration Act) (Law No. 224/1947),[76] if the family had been evacuated from the crescent-shaped evacuation zones around the crippled *Fukushima Dai'ichi* Nuclear Power Station, and for any home lost in its entirety. Families with a partially destroyed home were eligible for half of this sum (Brasor and Tsubuku 2011). This suggests that in relation to the allocation of charity money, the government framed home-owners rendered homeless by the disaster as among those in greatest need of assistance.

In addition to this private charity, the government also distributed disaster condolence money (*saigai chô'i-kin*, colloquially *mimai-kin*) of up to JPY five million to those who had lost close relatives in the disaster, pursuant to Article 3 of the Act on Provision of Disaster Condolence Grants etc. (Law No. 82/1973)[77] and municipal ordinances (Umeda 2013, p. 18). As additional measures, following calls for protection by the Bar, condolence grants and relief donations were exempted from seizure by creditors (*sashi'osae kinshi*, Article 5-2 of said act) and the scope of property not falling under bankrupt estates in cases of individual bankruptcy of disaster victims pursuant to Article 34 of the Bankruptcy Act (Law No. 75/2004)[78] was to be expanded (JFBA 2011a, p. 64, d, p. 12; Yamanome 2012; Katô 2013).

---

[75] On the role of donations, see Aota (2011).

[76] *Koseki-hô.*

[77] *Saigai chô'i-kin no shikyû-tô ni kansuru hôritsu.*

[78] *Hasan-hô.*

3.5 Housing Aid, Government Loans and Subsidies

The Government also acted as a direct provider of disaster-risk finance, more on the fiscal aspects of which is the subject matter of Chap. 2 in this volume. Regarding social welfare, the Act on Support for Reconstructing Livelihoods of Disaster Victims provides for two different grants for lost homes by the central and prefectural governments of up to JPY three million per household, Article 3 Section 4, from a designated public corporation, Article 6.[79]

The first, fundamental grant depends on the degree of damage to the respective residence, which, in quickened procedures, was distributed in lump sums of JPY one or a half million on an alternative basis, Article 3 para 2 of the act. The decisive test was essentially whether the respective building was either "completely destroyed" (*zenkai*, Article 2 para 2 No. 1) or suffered at least "large-scale partial damage" (*dai-kibô hankai*, Article 2 para 2 No. 2)—arbitrary standards difficult to construe in a non-discriminatory way.[80] The assessment of eligibility, the so-called damage certification (*higai nintei*), is conducted by land and house investigators, who, as a consequence, are now following revised guidelines, which operate on a percentage system to assess the extent of damage to walls, roof and foundation, granting aid if the total damage is deemed to exceed 40%.

The second, additional grant mostly depends on whether the victims purchase a new home (JPY two million), repair their home (one million) or rent private accommodation (a half million), Article 3 para 2 Nos. 1, 2, 3. Such a scheme clearly incentivises relocation and it can be argued that, considering the relatively low grant for renting, the poorest end up receiving the least.[81] On the other hand, as a means of disaster housing assistance, public guarantees that rents are "reimbursed for two years, typically up to a maximum of JPY 90,000" per month were granted initially, but there is "anxiety as to how long these subsidies will last." (Gill et al. 2013b, p. 10).

Thirdly, subsidies for participation in voluntary group relocations were introduced in the Act on Special Financial Support for Promoting Group Relocation for Disaster Mitigation (Law No. 132/1972).[82] Under this scheme, some 75–85% of pre-disaster property values are reimbursed upon agreement to relocate to safer, yet often remote areas far inland, complemented by interest subsidies.[83] However, accepting the subsidies excludes the grants for repairs outlined above, and thus entails the tough choice between onsite restoration, onsite reconstruction, or relocation and new construction,

[79]See generally Tsukui (2011).

[80]For details, see Brasor and Tsubuku (2011).

[81]According to the results of a comparative study of housing-problems after six earthquakes worldwide, renters generally "cannot afford the increase in market rents after the disaster and do not qualify for the permanent-housing subsidies aimed at homeowners" Johnson (2007, p. 454). For critical remarks, see Part 3.6(e).

[82]*Bôsai no tame no shûdan iten sokushin jigyô ni kakawaru kuni no zaisei-jô no tokubetsu sochi-tô ni kansuru hôritsu*; on the specific subsidies in Sendai, see Kabashima (2012, p. 11).

[83]For criticism, however, see Kabashima (2012, p. 11, p. 15).

particularly for double-loan victims.[84] Relocation is slowed down by the reluctance of "double debtors" to abandon and sell their former estates, who often would be better advised "to rebuild a simple house on their own land" in the absence of sufficient financial incentives to participate in group relocations.[85] In such cases, "agreement among stakeholders is time consuming, which prolongs residents' stays in temporary housing (…) well past the scheduled two-year period." (Cho 2014, pp. 168–169).[86] As relocation planning is in part marginalising the interests of double debtors, further assistance is deemed necessary for smooth implementation of the relocation (Kabashima 2012, pp. 14–15).[87]

Other financial benefits were provided by the Central Government on an emergency basis (Article 23 para 1 No. 7; 2 Disaster Relief Act) and at the discretion of the prefectural governments (Article 23 para 2; 2 Disaster Relief Act) (Law No. 108/1947).[88] These include public disbursements for overdue earned wages to save an estimated 30,000 jobs by use of JPY 700 billion of a first supplementary budget for subsidising salaries. To aid victims of the triple disaster, the Central Government and the local public entities (*chihô kôkyô dantai*), according to their responsibilities set forth in the Disaster Counter-measures Basic Act (Law No. 223/1961),[89] implemented emergency measures, some of which can be categorized as one of the relief activities listed in Article 23 para 1 Nos. 1–10 of the Disaster Relief Act.

Survivors rendered homeless by the tsunami or the earthquake assembled in emergency shelters and evacuation centres (*shinsai hinan-jo*).[90] Gradually, accommodation was provided by the government,[91] in accordance with Articles 2, 23 para 1 No. 1 of the Disaster Relief Act.[92] In addition, equipment, materials, and funding to maintain livelihoods was distributed pursuant to No. 7 of said paragraph, and ad hoc support was granted by the municipalities for emergency repairs to housing, pursuant to No. 6 of said paragraph. As with the case after the 1995 Kobe earthquake, a reconstruction fund set up after the catastrophe allows for support for the reconstruction of housing (*jûtaku saiken shi'en*) by providing subsidised low-interest loans for reconstruction, lease, etc. (Aota et al. 2010, p. 34; Edgington 2010, p. 87; Aota 2011, pp. 91–92; Ôno 1996, p. 27; Murosaki 2013, p. 110), accompanied by very limited relief for repairs, reconstruction, and rent. This was provided for in new legislation known as the Act on Support for Reconstructing Livelihoods of Disaster Victims

[84]See Torihata (2012, pp. 195–200) on further aspects of these problems in Miyagi and Iwate Prefectures.

[85]For details, see Kabashima (2012, pp. 10–11, pp. 13–14).

[86]See also Claremont (2014, p. 96).

[87]Or metaphorically put: "The people who really need to move now are the politicians and administrators who hold the purse strings for aid," Wilhelm and Delaney (2013, p. 122).

[88]*Saigai kyûjo-hô*; see Umeda (2013, pp. 6–7).

[89]*Saigai taisaku kihon-hô*; see Inaba (2011, pp. 22–23), Umeda (2013, pp. 4–6).

[90]These are usually schools or community centres. For captivating accounts, see e.g. Gill et al. (2013a); on the distinction between emergency and temporary shelters, temporary housing, and permanent housing, see e.g. Johnson (2007, pp. 436–437).

[91]On the selection of victims and the process of relocation, see Kitamura (2011, p. 55).

[92]See Kitamura (2011, pp. 46–51) for legal details and eligibility requirements.

(Law No. 66/1998).[93] Yet in practice, money for repairs was limited to a mere JPY 520,000, only to be used for rooms indispensable for daily life, e.g. living rooms, kitchens and bathrooms, subject to household income as well as damage sustained, and what is more, unavailable to all those seeking to occupy temporary housing.[94]

Ordinary unemployment benefits were increased to 50–80% (normally 60%) for 90 to a maximum of 330 days (normally 150), depending on age and individual entitlements under the national unemployment scheme of Articles 13–22 Employment Insurance Act (Law No. 116/1974).[95] In addition to general public benefits pursuant to, inter alia, the Livelihood Protection Act (Law No. 144/1950),[96] victims may apply for specific disaster benefits, such as exemptions from income tax for disaster-losses and from vehicle acquisition tax for replaced cars,[97] public health insurance payments, nursing care, high school fees, and special payments to farmers and fishermen (Brasor and Tsubuku 2011; Government of Japan, Cabinet Office 2011a, p. 23, b, p. 8). As necessary documents had often been lost, victims were provided with special identification certificates (*risai shômei-sho*). However, these financial recourses for victims must be applied for and filed separately, and with the municipal offices in the pre-disaster places of residence, which poses time-consuming practical hurdles.[98]

Government loan schemes are numerous and vary depending on their purpose and the municipalities in charge. In theory, any Japanese may obtain loans from the Japan Housing Finance Agency (JHFA), currently at a mere 1.47% for 35 years and 0% for disaster-affected homeowners—but this requires collateral. Disaster victim support loans are provided for persons below certain income levels by means of interest-free governmental and institutionalised loans or interest subsidies, see Article 23 para 1 Nos. 7, 2 Disaster Relief Act; Article 10 Act on Provision of Disaster Condolence Grants etc. Exceptions for the disaster of 2011 stretch the repayment period to 13 years.[99] Over 30 municipal councils providing social welfare pay up to JPY 200,000 per month in no-interest loans to victims who have lost their jobs, as well as households who have lost a family member.[100] These so-called "life and welfare loans" do not require a guarantor or any repayment within the first year, but fall due after the second year.

Single mothers, widows and orphans are eligible for other no-interest loans from a fund for moving, repairs, medical care, and education (Umeda 2013, p. 19). Specific

---

[93]*Hisai-sha seikatsu saiken shi'en-hô*; on the enactment and subsequent amendments, see Yagi (2007), Deguchi (2014), and Part 2.9.

[94]For critical remarks, see Part 3.1.

[95]*Koyô hoken-hô*; for details, see Umeda (2013, p. 21).

[96]*Seikatsu hogo-hô*; for a critical overview of the laws and social policies for homeless people, see Iwata (2007, pp. 152–162).

[97]For statutory details, see Umeda (2013, p. 20).

[98]See Brasor and Tsubuku (2011); on some legal solutions, see Umeda (2013, pp. 16–17).

[99]JPY 640.7 billion was allocated for this in the first supplementary budget alone. see also Japan Press Weekly (2011a), Umeda (2013, p. 19).

[100]See also Mainichi Daily News (2011).

low-interest loans are available to persons engaged in agricultural or fisheries industries (Government of Japan, Cabinet Office 2011a, p. 23). In Sendai, for example, five-year no-interest housing loans of JPY 11.6 million are available from the local government for people working in agriculture of fisheries (Kabashima 2012, p. 11, p. 13)—short in comparison to the 20 years usually necessary to pay off a home in Japan. It is highly questionable as to whether all this is sufficient for a new home, as in Tôhoku, a home constructed on one's own land can cost up to an estimated JPY 30 million or JPY 10 million on rented land—between three and ten times more than the value of the two grants.[101] Another alleged problem is that, even if double-loan debtors receive governmental loan guarantees, they are still obliged to secure the loan with property (Brasor and Tsubuku 2011). This has led some to conclude that neither the government loans nor the relocation subsidies cater adequately for the specific and exacerbated situation of home-owners,[102] leaving their situation largely unremedied.

4 Discussion of the Responses to Disaster-Induced Financial Distress

To summarise, despite the trillions of yen spent on recovery, tireless statutory activity and an impressive array of law and policy measures directly or indirectly mitigating damage from the disaster, a truly helpful solution for double-loans remains missing. Except for emergency relief for repairs, insufficient housing grants conflicting with relocation subsidies, counselling, and unsuccessful guidelines for liquidation, little is in place to keep double-loan debtors from slipping through the wide-meshed safety net of inadequate earthquake insurance and restrained social security. Double-loans, being at the intersection of disaster management, debtor-creditor- and real property-law, financial regulation, and social welfare, pose a significant test for social justice in Japan, and the degree to which society accepts financial responsibility for victims of natural disasters.

Therefore, in this section we turn to a critical and normative assessment of the results of the laws enacted and policies adopted. Whilst the need for the government to provide housing and reconstruction aid following disasters is now generally accepted, a failure to address the social disaster of lost homes and double-loans as well as the need for additional debt relief have produced instances of evident inefficiencies and social injustice. This inadequacy has been compounded by a social discourse on the topic of social justice post disasters, that whilst outspoken has been severely limited in scope. By way of conclusion, we argue that too much focus in these debates has

[101] The average price of a Japanese condominium (*manshon*) was JPY 51 million in 2014, and although property in the rural Tôhoku region is much cheaper, typical two-bedroom apartments with a kitchen, living and dining room (*2LDK*) are only available for around JPY 700,000 in coastal Ishinomaki City, for example.

[102] See Kabashima (2012, p. 14).

been put on issues of pre-disaster vulnerability and responsibility. Hence, we contend that not enough concern has been paid to individuals' post-disaster circumstances and the threats these pose to their ability to function in society, leading to the unfolding social disaster of double-loans.

4.1 Limited Effectiveness and Efficiency

Japan made considerable progress in rehousing the half-million people left without homes in March 2011—they have found shelter, rubble has been cleared, roads have been rebuilt, and public services have resumed.[103] Measures included the procurement and erection of 72,000 prefabricated, trailer-like units of emergency temporary housing (*ôkyû kasetsu jûtaku*) and provisional relocation to private rental apartments, government employees' housing, local governmental public housing, employment promotion housing, hotels and inns—partly allocated by lottery, by way of group relocation (*shûdan iten*), and according to tough eligibility requirements, very much dependent on the municipality in charge (Government of Japan, Cabinet Office 2011b, p. 7).[104]

Yet, in construing articles 1 and 2 of the Basic Act on Reconstruction in Response to the Great East Japan Earthquake (Law No. 76/2011),[105] the legislators' ultimate intent was, rather explicitly, "the revitalisation of Japan, not the restoration of victims' lives," so that national economic growth was prioritized over disaster recovery. As for prefectural recovery plans, similar priority was observed to be given to economic growth in favour of community reconstruction (Cho 2014, p. 172). In this way, a dichotomy between the physical concept of "reconstruction" (*fukkô*) and a more anthropocentric concept of "rebuilding" people's lives (*saiken*) becomes apparent: In contrast to the swift restoration of public physical infrastructure—roads, bridges, gas and power lines—progress and implementation of onsite reconstruction housing (*fukkô jûtaku*) or permanent relocation of coastal communities has been criticised as slow (Gill et al. 2013b, pp. 9–11; Cho 2014, pp. 161–163, p. 165, p. 173); Claremont 2014, p. 95).

This slowness has not always resulted from market failures. For instance, housing reconstruction in Tôhoku was generally driven much more by the government than by the market or charity; meaning that government policies are largely responsible for delayed or failed recovery.[106] From a fiscal perspective, many victims who lost their homes were unable to benefit from national reconstruction grants (*fukkô kôfukin*) to

---

[103] See generally Wakabayashi et al. (2011).

[104] See again Kitamura (2011, pp. 53–57). Due to vague national criteria, eligibility for temporary housing significantly differed among the municipalities, whereas after the Kobe earthquake, priority for placement was explicitly given to the elderly, the disabled, single parents, and low-income households, Johnson (2007, p. 445).

[105] *Higashi-nihon dai-shinsai fukkô kihon-hô*; English transl. available online: http://www.reconstruction.go.jp/english/topics/Basic_Act_on_Reconstruction.pdf.

[106] See Cho (2014, p. 173), Kennedy et al. (2008) on how to "build back better" after a tsunami.

a large extent, due to their delayed and limited allocation to the municipalities and their prevalent use for public infrastructure (Cho 2014, pp. 165–166; Claremont 2014, p. 95). To the outrage of many, it was revealed that "one quarter of the reconstruction budget has been spent on projects that arguably have little or nothing to do with reconstruction of the affected areas." (Claremont 2014, p. 95).[107] Finally, it was prolonged budgetary uncertainty about the provision of grants to municipalities (Cho 2014, pp. 164–165), subsidies to companies, and aid to victims that left reconstruction in limbo.

As a result of these institutional weaknesses, 89,000 evacuees still remained in temporary accommodation across the three most affected prefectures by August 2014, long after the end of the two-year maximum stay prescribed by law, while 90,000 lived in units rented temporarily by local governments (Ishibashi 2014). When we last went to the Tôhoku area for fieldwork in late 2016, we still observed unresolved cases of double-loan-induced homelessness, such as a family of five in the fishing town of Yuri'age, Natori City, whose affected property was bought by the municipality at a price seven times lower than the original value, as prices were set based on the property values after the decision to change the zoning. Some elderly evacuees in temporary housing remain reluctant to move out of their containers at all, as rents on the private market seem too high, or moving into reconstruction housing would perpetuate the loss of communal ties. Vulnerability and resilience vary from community to community, and between urban and rural regions, but most of the tsunami victims still in temporary housing are completely unable to afford the rents and are simply waiting for public social housing, construction of which will not be completed before the end of 2017 (Ishibashi 2014). While an all-time low in mortgage rates may have spurred construction in 2015 (after a drop due to the increased consumption tax), the market has been unable to supply homes affordable to indebted disaster victims.

The government has also offered no holistic legal approach to tackling issues of debt relief,[108] and as we saw in Sects. 3.1–3.5, the numerous, yet partial solutions to these problems often failed to work as intended. The loans and disbursements could not provide a substitute for disaster insurance, let alone full compensation for lost homes. On the one hand, the affected financial institutions have been supported with billions of yen and disaster-hit companies have been bailed out by the government whilst, on the other hand, public short-term and private high-interest loans, temporary debt-freezes and charity donations postpone rather than prevent insolvencies of the

[107]Nevertheless, partial use of the grants for clearance and disposal of debris, reallocation of land to relocate housing and so forth might have at least helped the victims indirectly.

[108]The multi-faceted crisis has also been dealt with by different ministries, which took different stances on the way to respond: For example, the Ministries responsible for government-affiliated financial institutions, such as the Ministry of Economy, Trade and Industry, the Ministry of Land, Infrastructure, Transport and Tourism, and the Ministry of Agriculture, Forestry and Fisheries, unlike the Ministry of Finance, which does not have authority over policy-based finance, could arrange for public zero-interest loan schemes, see Financial Services Agency (2011c).

private double-loan victims. Given the insufficiency of the housing grants, instead, a system that can financially and sustainably cover evacuee life was demanded.[109]

In June 2011, the Cabinet Office vaguely communicated a planned policy regarding double-loans to financial institutions in which "the national and local governments, lenders and borrowers [must] share the pain."[110] What this was to mean in practice, however, was that in addition to bailing out companies as "gifts" to creditor institutions, the government did more to mitigate or offset the lenders' losses than to help the borrowers. The reluctance to tackle double-loan problems head-on was explained by the Minister of Finance, highlighting legal concerns about debt relief in light of the protection of property under the Japanese Constitution: As "private-sector financial institutions use private deposits (…) as source of funds for the provision of loans," in granting debt release, the government, he implied, would infringe upon depositors' property rights.[111] While post-disaster debt release has also been portrayed as difficult from the perspective of private and public financial discipline,[112] some scholars have been equally restrictive, contending that "loan write-off shall never be used" as this may jeopardize the affected institutions' viability and would "not benefit non-borrowing victims."[113] It is highly probable that the government's decision to actively support affected financial institutions rather than their debtors was rooted in similar considerations.[114]

For example, the FSA introduced exceptions to the Act on Special Measures for Strengthening Financial Functions (Law No. 128/2004),[115] inter alia making affected credit cooperatives (*shin'yô kyôdô kumi'ai*), Shinkin Banks (*shin'yô kinko*), and regional banks (*chihô ginkô*) eligible for public subsidies to offset losses incurred as a result of personal and corporate borrowers' defaults (Ohira and Chiba 2011; Ranghieri and Ishiwatari 2014, p. 275).[116] Accordingly, the government decided to inject the impressive sum of JPY 191 billion, as of March 30, 2012 "under very favourable conditions," into ten of these institutions, and has continued to advance more until 2017 (Ranghieri and Ishiwatari 2014, p. 275).

Another example of assistance to the financial sector—the deregulation of further lending described above—drew heavy criticism. Instead of attempting to resurrect the loan sharks by means of eradicating consumer protection, NPOs and the left-wing media mobilised for loan forgiveness and an increase in financial disaster aid

[109] See e.g. Yamasaki (2003, p. 91).

[110] Transl. by Umeda (2013, p. 19).

[111] This legal line of argument invokes that a "haircut" to the creditor's claims would constitute an outright expropriation of their property rights, see Financial Services Agency (2011b).

[112] See Financial Services Agency (2011b).

[113] See Anand Kumar and Newport (2005, p. 178).

[114] Japan's previous financial crises demonstrate a long history of bank bailouts for bad-loan problems, from the rescues by the Ministry of Finance after the steep drop in real estate prices of 1991 and 1993, followed by the 1995 total collapse of *jûsen* companies—mortgage lending institutions created by banks in the 1970s.

[115] *Kin'yû kinô no kyôka no tame no tokubetsu sochi ni kan suru hôritsu*; the amendment partially revising this act was by Law No. 80/2011.

[116] For details, see Torihata (2012, pp. 204–206).

under the Act on Support for Reconstructing Livelihoods of Disaster Victims[117]: As criticised with regard to other Japanese post-disaster legislation, "adjustments (…) need to be made on a temporary basis for the good of the people in rebuilding, and not as a backdoor way to change the law for the benefit of a few (…)." (Wilhelm and Delaney 2013, p. 122). After prolonging the FSA's exceptional rules once, which would well support Naomi Klein's controversial theory that disasters are often used as pretexts for deregulation,[118] it is noteworthy that the lending deregulation has indeed been withdrawn as of 31 March 2012. It remains unclear for whom exactly the amendments had been thought necessary in the first place, and whether the FSA subsequently backpedalled in belated comprehension that facilitating lending to over-indebted disaster victims is little different from throwing oil on the fire.

The government's half-hearted reactions to double-loans and debt relief can be seen to follow what has been distilled as general rationales of financial disaster relief in Japan: "compensate if the law requires, but not otherwise; compensate symbolically, but not enough to truly cover losses; compensate uniformly, but not tailored to individual loss." (Feldman 2013, pp. 336–340, p. 355).[119] In one of the world's wealthiest countries, part of what made agreement on financial relief difficult is rooted in questions of disaster justice.

4.2 Social Justice and Social Injustice

In discussing social justice issues in relation to disaster recovery it can be helpful to distinguish three different ways in which disaster-related injustice, including that of the double-loans crisis, can be framed. On the first, distributive framing, the victims are seen as vulnerable persons, many of whom being amongst the worst-off groups in Japan, unable to take responsibility for recovering from the disaster without external assistance. On this framing, relief is owed as a means of responding to a general duty of benevolence, to promote equity and alleviate suffering in society. On the second, rectificatory framing, the 'victims' of the double-loan crisis can be said to have been specifically harmed by government failures and inactivity, from a failure to prevent the damage caused by the disaster by adequate coastal zoning laws and a failure to provide reconstruction and rehabilitation in a timely manner to a failure to provide functional financial opportunities for them to achieve financial and social security. Relief is then said to be owed by the state as a matter of rectification for this past injustice. On the final, precautionary framing, people are the victims of two disasters, the first of which having been caused by the 'natural' earthquake and

[117]See Japan Press Weekly (2011a).

[118]In "The Shock Doctrine: The Rise of Disaster Capitalism," Klein critically observes that disasters are regularly followed by imposing deregulation, privatisation, and cuts to social spending so swiftly that victims and other stakeholders have no chance to oppose. In this way, crises are seen to be exploited to push through controversial, exploitative policies while citizens are too emotionally and physically distracted, see Klein (2008).

[119]Here, "compensation" does not refer to tort law.

tsunami, and the second, social disaster, being caused by the preventable economic and social consequences of this first disaster. On this framing, relief should be given as a means of avoiding the second disaster, just as tsunami walls and other measures were taken in order to try and prevent the first, natural disaster, and hence preventing this avoidable harm.[120]

The Japanese political debate about public responsibility to the victims of the Great East Japan Disaster[121] quickly turned to discussions on the issue of double-loans. This discourse, on the whole, considered double-loans mostly from a distributive perspective, without implying responsibility by the government for causing the disaster or considering ways of preventing future harm. Calls for appropriate policies to allocate resources to certain vulnerable groups[122] were soon to be heard. Politicians such as the Mayor of Minami-Sanriku City, two consecutive Ministers of Finance, the Governor of the Bank of Japan and the Prime Minister equally expressed their concerns over double-loans,[123] but disagreement arose over who was most affected, what weight was to be attached to their losses, and thus who was to be deemed in need and worthy of financial assistance. In the disaster zone, victims of double-loans were certainly not the only ones in need.[124] Social inequality affected various groups framed as vulnerable (*zeijaku*), ranging from the poor, elderly, isolated, and disabled, to precarious contract workers at the crippled nuclear power plant.[125] Particularly "weak groups" among disaster victims are framed by the term *saigai jakusha*, officially used in plans for persons requiring assistance at times of disaster (*saigai-ji yô-engo-sha*), such as women and children, which are explicitly listed in the Basic Act on Reconstruction in Response to the Great East Japan Earthquake.

The government's costly disaster response raises its own questions on distributive justice, i.e. notions of "fair" allocation of costs and resources for disaster recovery among the members of society.[126] Whilst there are many differing notions of distributive justice, it is generally recognised that the distribution of goods should be both egalitarian and responsible to individual choices and decisions (Dworkin 2002, p. 74). On one famous account, these competing desiderata are brought together in the view that "It is bad—unjust and unfair—for some to be worse off than others through no fault [or choice] of their own." (Temkin 1993, p. 13). Distributional injustice after a disaster, in this sense, arises if one group of victims is perceived to have received too little benefit, relative to their need, or to bear too much burden, relative to what they deserve. Justice, being "the first virtue of social institutions," (Rawls 1999, p. 3) thus depends on the conception of how to compare those affected by a disaster,

---

[120]This three-fold division represents three general categories of social justice and reflects other, similar divisions within the domain of justice, for instance, the distinction between the purposes of tort law, or between the moral duties of fidelity, beneficence and care.

[121]See e.g. Feldman (2013, p. 339).

[122]See e.g. Cho (2014, p. 174).

[123]See Financial Services Agency (2011b), Shûkan Kin'yû Zaisei Jijô (2011).

[124]See the distinction between the groups of *higai-sha*, *hisai-sha*, and *hinan-sha* in Sect. 1.

[125]See Cho (2014, pp. 169–171, p. 173, p. 174), Claremont (2014, p. 96).

[126]See generally Kabashima (2012).

so that everyone receives their fair share of government aid. Criteria for distribution fundamentally differ in the way in which they construe fairness, depending on the respective "substantive values underlying the distribution," such as merit and equity, equality, or individual need.[127] While interest in the topic of "disaster justice"[128] is growing globally, concepts of vulnerability, referring to "states of susceptibility to harm, powerlessness, and marginality of both physical and social systems," guide the resulting normative actions for disaster victims (Adger 2006, p. 268).

Compared with this emerging, if contested, discourse on distributive justice, the Japanese government has been far more resistant to discussions of disaster responsibility, blame, and the possibility that relief is owed as a means of rectification for avoidable government failures, drawing a strong distinction between the "natural" earthquake and tsunami and the "man-made" nuclear accident as distinct elements of the 3/11 triple disaster.[129] However, this narrative of government blamelessness over the death and destruction caused by the natural disaster was not uncontested, with some still framing the earthquake and tsunami as "man-made" catastrophes, at least in part, for instance regarding the under-insurance of homeowners, inadequate urban planning, the failure to evacuate children on time, and the insufficient tsunami walls in several coastal municipalities. As victims gradually shifted their attention from loss and urgent needs to the politics of the re-construction priorities, they voiced strong criticism about radiation safety levels and the selective plans for the permanent relocation of communities away from the shore and the crippled Fukushima power plant.[130]

However, such discourses were limited to local cases and did not reach a national scale, just as they also did not trigger large demonstrations in Tokyo or blaming as in the case of the nuclear accident. As Japan had already been "one of the world's most prepared nations in dealing with natural disasters, experts and policy makers have been struggling to answer" how it could have been more resilient and better prepared.[131] Thus, even if one accepted the notion that some of the victims of the earthquake and the tsunami were harmed by government failure, it was much harder to identify these victims, or how the government could have served them better, than it was with regard to the Fukushima Dai'ichi Nuclear Disaster.

The failure of these two kinds of public discourses to achieve any meaningful shift towards a more just response to disaster recovery or to prevent the emerging double-loan crisis—because equality can be seen as demanding equal treatment of all disaster victims while agency in natural disasters is hard to prove—indicates the difficulty in forming a robust conception of social justice that can be applied to complex disasters. Both discourses on social justice that emerged in Japan following

---

[127]See fundamentally Deutsch (1985, pp. 2–3, pp. 38–45) and the contributions in Fourie et al. (2015).

[128]For an authoritative overview, see Verchick (2012).

[129]The following is based on Hörhager and Weitzdörfer (forthcoming), where further references can be found.

[130]Again, see Cho (2014).

[131]For suggestions to improve resilience, see Shimizu (2012, p. 40), Ranghieri and Ishiwatari (2014).

the disaster required the framing of a class of victims deserving of relief, and such framings can easily undermine the case for more robust action on behalf of the government rather than promoting it.

This can be seen in the following five practical dilemmas of disaster aid: (a) *Tsunami Victims versus Nuclear Victims*: Victims harmed by the nuclear accident have enjoyed the benefits of actual legal rights in tort, at least in theory covering the full value of the real property before contamination,[132] yet appear no more "worthy" of relief than the victims of the "natural" tsunami. (b) *Insured Victims vs. Uninsured Victims*: Insurance is usually seen as providing autonomy in the face of risk as, "the decision to buy or reject (…) insurance is a calculated gamble." (Dworkin 2002, p. 74). However, in the world's most earthquake-prone country, this kind of autonomy seems unrealistic. There are simply too many institutional barriers to greater insurance uptake, including the fact that indemnity insurance for natural disaster cannot be taken out against the full cost of disaster damage, was not sensitive to risk at the sub-prefecture level, is only available when packaged with fire insurance, and is vulnerable to seizure by mortgagees, without mortgagees placing any obligation on lenders to be insured. Yet, despite such barriers, considerations of merit and governance render it difficult to privilege double-loan victims over those who have paid costly premiums for decades, and this would further disincentivise taking out insurance in the future. (c) *Large, Corporate Debt versus Small, Private Debt*: It is highly likely that if larger "enterprises go bankrupt and fail, local industries will be irreparably damaged and many local workers will lose their jobs." (Katô 2013). Yet relief to larger corporations carries the risk of assisting the wealthy who stand to gain most from them. (d) *Debtors versus Creditors*: Perhaps the most difficult aspect of disaster justice is rooted in the fact that double-loan problems were predictable for creditors as well as for debtors. For a long time, Japanese institutional lenders had been aware that in relation to mortgaged loans, "the highest risk is the condemnation through physical damages caused by earthquake, typhoon or other acts of god." (AES Ltd. 2005). However, responsibility for insurance generally falls upon the debtor, on the grounds that they are seen to have been most able to avoid risks, by not seeking the loan in the first place or by influencing the exposure of their chosen collateral. (e) *Home-owners versus Renters*: Finally, home-owners have been treated more favourably and more generously than renters, for instance regarding the distribution of charity money and housing grants described above. However, in disaster research it is often the tenants that are framed as a population more vulnerable and as "most in need of temporary housing." (Johnson 2007, p. 456).

Given this failure of victim-based approaches to disaster justice, we therefore conclude that a forward-looking, "precautionary" approach to post disaster justice may be more appropriate for a large-scale disaster such as the 3/11 tsunami. Let us now examine some suggestions for moving towards such an approach.

---

[132]On these principles and the challenges of nuclear liability, see e.g. Weitzdörfer (2014).

4.3 Suggestions for Improvement

The first author visited Japan not long after the 1995 Great Hanshin Earthquake (M 7.2, causing 6,434 casualties), experienced the 2004 Chûetsu Earthquake first-hand (M 6.9, 40 casualties) while on a trip to the area, was shaken in the 2007 Chûetsu Offshore Earthquake while working on the twelfth floor of a law-office in Tokyo (M 6.6, causing 11 casualties and a minor nuclear accident at *Kashiwazaki-Kariwa*), and returned in 2011 to conduct legal research after the Great East Japan Earthquake (M 9.0, almost 19,000 casualties). Literally on the day this paragraph was drafted in 2014, landslides in Hiroshima Prefecture claimed the lives of more than 70 people. Only weeks later, volcanic eruptions on Mount Ontake killed at least 57, and another 50 were killed by the 2016 Kumamoto earthquakes (M 7.0). This permanence of cataclysm demonstrates that in the "Earthquake Nation"[133] of Japan (*jishin-koku de aru nihon*), society will always have to face disasters—and law will always be needed to cope with these disasters.

Yet, neither legal claims nor charity can substitute for the loss of a family home or birthplace. They cannot compensate for the support of human ties and community, let alone a lost relative or friend. Along the narrow coastlines, there is literally limited room left for stricter zoning rules or for providing higher standards in the built infrastructure. New gigantic seawalls, up to 15 m high and planned to cover over 400 km of shore are known to have failed previously, create false perceptions of safety, and obstruct tourism and fishery. As with the costly coastal defences, it is for experts to decide whether three first and newly enacted laws on tsunamis, among them the Act on the Promotion of Tsunami Counter-mea-sures (Law No. 77/2011)[134] (its bill previously abandoned in 2010), will improve resilience through enhanced zoning, research, education and evacuation training (Umeda 2013, pp. 46–47). Certainly, it is often more efficient to reduce hazard risk by addressing socioeconomic vulnerability instead of pouring concrete (Verchick 2012, p. 51).[135]

Whilst criticising governments for insufficient, inadequate or unjust disaster response is a simple exercise, it is important to consider the enormous challenges a compound disaster like 3/11 brings about. In addition, a complex socioeconomic problem like the double-loan crisis, given the unchangeable geological conditions of Japan, can hardly be addressed with simple solutions, and most schemes in place will have to be retained and incrementally improved to best combine ex-ante and ex-post measures of disaster risk governance and financing.

We assert that social justice, at least in its precautionary role, also has a key role to play in post-disaster finance. Such an approach starts from the premise that in a complex and interdependent society with mature financial institutions, the knock-on effects of disasters on the economy, and in particular on the financial position of those affected, will be difficult to contain. Victims who are in debt cannot help but either be forced deeper into debt or be denied access to much needed capital, and will

[133]In English, this term was also coined by Clancey (2006, p. 6, 226 et seq.).

[134]*Tsunami taisaku no suishin ni kansuru hôritsu.*

[135]Aldrich (2012) argues that social capital is key to building resilience.

either be made bankrupt or prevented from playing a productive role in social and economic reconstruction. Whatever the outcome of such dilemmas, they will only have additional knock-on effects for society at large, prompting the kind of social disaster typified by Japan's double-loan crisis.

Whilst such knock-on effects may not be easily calculable, they are predictable. We therefore believe that governments are under a duty to seek to avoid them as a precaution to protect the citizens. Such precautionary measures have already been taken very seriously by the government when it comes to the physical infrastructure and the science of natural disasters ever since the *Nôbi* earthquake of 1891, when it established the world's first interdisciplinary disaster research body, turning Japan into a leader in seismology.[136] Yet, a concern for the predictable and avoidable social consequences of such disasters has remained undeveloped.

There is a growing body of law on the prevention principle and the precautionary principle in environmental law as well as in health and safety law around the world, operating alongside traditional notions of equity, responsibility and social justice. We contend that the time is ripe to transpose and implement these principles in disaster justice and disaster law, especially when it comes to post-disaster relief.

To this extent, we note the adoption of the Sendai Framework for Disaster Risk Reduction in 2015.[137] To strengthen disaster risk governance, Article 30 explicitly states the need

> (j) To strengthen the design and implementation of inclusive policies and social safety-net mechanisms, including through community involvement, integrated with livelihood enhancement programmes (…), housing and education, towards the eradication of poverty, to find durable solutions in the post-disaster phase and to empower and assist people disproportionately affected by disasters; (m) To promote, as appropriate, the integration of disaster risk reduction considerations and measures in financial and fiscal instruments; (g) To promote and support the development of social safety nets as disaster risk reduction measures linked to and integrated with livelihood enhancement programmes in order to ensure resilience to shocks at the household and community levels; (…).

Despite its developed economy, legal and scientific sophistication and indeed economic and social equality, Japan has a comparatively underdeveloped social security system. It therefore seems that meeting these objectives will require developing more robust safety nets for the victims of disasters, based around identifying obstacles to their rehabilitation following a disaster, as well as the need to alleviate both immediate and on-going suffering.

In the absence of a full-fledged social welfare system, few better legal remedies than insurance, a well-tried risk-sharing arrangement, with Japan already hovering between a privately and publicly funded system (Kozuka 2012, pp. 5–6, pp. 90–93), seem to be at hand. Private insurance for earthquakes, tsunami and volcanic eruptions is heavily subsidised by the government, but not intended to cover entire

---

[136]The Imperial Earthquake Investigation Committee (*Shinsai yobô chôsa-kai*), see Clancey (2006, p. 151).

[137]The Sendai Framework for Disaster Risk Reduction (2015–2030), adopted by 187 UN member states in 2015, constitutes the most comprehensive risk management framework.

losses.[138] In light of the enormous catastrophic risk in Japan, this market would not exist without subsidies and restrictions on insurers' exposure.[139] Thus, only 30–50% of the net value of a property can be insured, and this is capped at JPY 50 million for homes and JPY ten million for household property under Article 2 para 2 No. 4 of the Act on Earthquake Insurance (Law No. 73/1966).[140] As a means of simplifying the claims process, payments are either the full amount, half, or 5% of the amount insured (Kozuka 2012, p. 5).

Neither creditors nor debtors appear to have been very risk averse with regard to insurance. Creditors did not frequently insist on the conclusion of insurance contracts for mortgaged property, whilst most debtors did not take it out.[141] Home-owners were and still are fatally reluctant to insure earthquake risks.[142] The reasons for this are disputed,[143] but, as described above, include many institutional barriers: insurance coverage is not mandatory and is only available as a supplement to fire insurance whilst insurance premiums are fixed for each prefecture and perceived as costly relative to incomes.[144] The penetration rate of earthquake insurance was as low as one third in the tsunami-prone prefecture of Miyagi (Kozuka 2012, p. 7).[145] Nevertheless, after the disaster, insurance was one of the major legal concerns discussed at counselling centres,[146] and within only eight months, JPY 1.18 trillion had been paid out on over 718,000 policies in Japan (Kozuka 2012, p. 7).

Although increased insurance coverage and the transfer of risks in exchange for premiums would improve risk management and significantly improve households' resilience,[147] the devil is in the detail. On the one hand, economists have shown that "insurance premiums convey risk information to potential buyers in the coastal housing market."[148] On the other hand, private prevention instead of taxpayer-funded disaster response is a slippery slope towards leaving the poor unprotected from disaster risk. We therefore propose that, whilst subsidies should be maintained, locally flexible risk-sensitive insurance premiums could signal warnings to the coastal and

---

138 See e.g. Yamamoto (2011, p. 74).

139 On the resilience of Japanese insurance companies to earthquakes, see Soichiro Moridaira, Chap. 5 of this volume.

140 *Jishin hôken ni kan suru hôritsu.*

141 For critical remarks, see Parts 3.6(b) and (c).

142 For details, see Waldenberger (2013), Kozuka (2012, p. 7), Feldman (2013, p. 339).

143 For an overview, see Waldenberger (2013).

144 See e.g. Dôjima hôritsu jimu-sho [Dôjima Law Office] (2011, pp. 218–220).

145 For more data, see Takahiro Tsuda, Chap. 2 of this volume.

146 See JFBA (2011a, p. 60).

147 See e.g. Dôjima hôritsu jimu-sho [Dôjima Law Office] (2011, pp. 218–220), Williams and Jacobs (2011, p. 191), Katô (2012), Ôgaki (2013), Waldenberger (2013). Japan's insurance penetration rate is increasing, particularly since 2011, yet still under 30% as of 2016, see also Takahiro Tsuda, Chap. 2 of this volume.

148 See e.g. Bin et al. (2008). Endeavouring to consider behavioural or cultural factors leading to ignorance of well-documented tsunami risks would go beyond the scope of this chapter; for a theoretical explanation, see e.g. Kunreuther and Pauly (2004).

wooden housing markets, to banks and potential mortgagors in particular, contributing necessary incentives to live in—where available—less popular, but safer locations. To improve penetration rates, one might decouple earthquake insurance from fire insurance, make it mandatory, or create an opt-out system, incentivising creditors to insist on insurance by putting future subsidies and bailouts under this condition, which dedicated chapters of this volume explore in more detail.

We also believe that allowing creditors to subrogate insurance pay-outs for mortgaged properties should be abolished, except in such cases where insurance either is paid for by the lender or is a compulsory condition of obtaining the mortgage. As a matter of justice, creditors should not have a prior claim to insurance pay-outs that have been freely obtained by property owners, and this fact is only emphasised when the debtor is in a financially stressed position such as following a natural disaster. As a matter of pure efficiency such a move would improve insurance uptake by making disaster insurance pay-outs more valuable to indebted property owners and encouraging lenders to require them more often.

We acknowledge that such measures could be costly to citizens. However, overall, they will likely prove less costly than the consequences of inaction, and they will likely be a very efficient means of allocating resources to promote faster and better recovery of communities and individual lives.

Acknowledgements This project at the Centre for the Study of Existential Risk, University of Cambridge, was made possible through the support of a grant from Templeton World Charity Foundation, Inc. The opinions expressed in this publication are those of the author(s) and do not necessarily reflect the views of Templeton World Charity Foundation, Inc. Previous work on this topic was funded by the Volkswagen Foundation, within its "Key Issues for Research and Society" initiative, through the research project "Protecting the Weak: Entangled Processes of Framing, Mobilization and Institutionalization in East Asia" (AZ 87382) at the Interdisciplinary Centre for East-Asian Studies, Goethe University Frankfurt/Main, and by the DIJ Tokyo through a visiting scholarship awarded to Julius Weitzdörfer.

References

Adachi I (2011) Higashi-nihon dai-shinsai ni tomonau nijû rôn mondai de 'kojin saimu-sha no shiteki seiri ni kan suru gaidorain' ga sakutei sareru ['Guidelines for individual debtor private liquidation' are stipulated for the double loan problem caused by the Great East Japan Earthquake]. New Bus Law 958:8–10

Adger WN (2006) Vulnerability. Glob Environ Change 16(3):268–281

AES Ltd (2005) Lending issues in Japan. Asset Enhancement Services Ltd. http://www.aes-intl.com/download/lendingissues.pdf

Aldrich DP (2012) Building resilience: social capital in post-disaster recovery. University of Chicago Press, Chicago

Anand Kumar TS, Newport JK (2005) Role of microfinance in disaster mitigation. Disaster Prev Manag 14:176–182 (2005). https://doi.org/10.1108/09653560510595173

Ando J, Shoda A, Yanagita M (2013) Still room to devise ways for loans to disaster-affected firms: ease double-loan burden with new lending methods. Japan Center for Economic Research. http://www.jcer.or.jp/eng/pdf/kinyu20130430.pdf

Aota R (2011) Hisai-sha shi'en ni kakaru saigai fukkô kikin to gi'en-kin no yakuwari ni kan suru kôsatsu (On the role of disaster recovery funds and donations to aid victims). Saigai Fukkô Kenkyû (Bull. Disaster Recovery) 3:87–117

Aota R, Murosaki Y, Hokugo A (2010) Saigai fukkô kikin to chûkan shi'en soshiki ga rendô shita ue de no chi'iki shudô ni yoru fukkô suishin no arikata ni kan suru kôsatsu (A study on the promotion of disaster recovery by local initiatives, on the basis of the relationship between the disaster recovery fund and intermediary organizations). In: Chi'iki Anzen Gakkai Kôgai-shû (Proceedings of the annual conference of the institute of social safety science), vol 12, pp 31–40

Bin O, Kruse JB, Landry CE (2008) Flood hazards, insurance rates, and amenities: evidence from the coastal housing market. J Risk Insur 75(1):63–82

Brasor P, Tsubuku M (2011) Let them rent mansions: compensation for disaster victims will barely make a difference. Jpn Times. http://blog.japantimes.co.jp/yen-for-living/let-them-rent-mansions-compensation-for-disaster-victims-will-barely-make-a-difference/

Butt S, Nasu H, Nottage L (eds) (2014) Asia-pacific disaster management: comparative and socio-legal perspectives. Springer, Berlin, Heidelberg

Cho A (2014) Post-tsunami recovery and reconstruction: governance issues and implications of the Great East Japan Earthquake. Disasters 38(s2):s157–s178

Citibank Japan (2011) To all victims of the Great East Japan Earthquake (on file with the authors). Citibank Japan. www.citibank.co.jp/en/customernotices

Clancey GK (2006) Earthquake nation: the cultural politics of Japanese seismicity, 1868–1930. University of California Press, Berkeley

Claremont Y (2014) Disaster in Japan: a case study. In: Butt S, Nasu H, Nottage L (eds) Asia-pacific disaster management: comparative and socio-legal perspectives. Springer, Berlin Heidelberg, pp 79–99

Deguchi S (2014) Seikatsu, jûtaku saiken o meguru rippô undô (Legislative activities concerning the reconstruction of housing and livelihoods). In Kansei gakuin daigaku saigai fukkô seido kenkyû-jo, Hisai-sha seikatsu saiken shi'en-hô kôka kenshô kenkyû-kai (Kwansei Gakuin University Institute for Disaster Recovery Systems, & Study Group for the Inspection of the effects of the Act on Support for Reconstructing Livelihoods of Disaster Victims) (eds), Kenshô hisai-sha seikatsu saiken shi'en-hô (Inspection of the Act on Support for Reconstructing Livelihoods of Disaster Victims), pp 109–135. Tokyo: Shizen saigai hisai-sha shi'en sokushin renraku-kai

Deutsch M (1985) Distributive justice: a social-psychological perspective. Yale University Press, New Haven

Dôjima hôritsu jimu-sho [Dôjima Law Office] (2011) Q&A shinsai to saiken kaishû tôsan taiô (Questions and answers: Debt collection, insolvency support and natural disaster), Tokyo, Shôji Hômu

Dôshita H (2012) Yami-kin'yû no higai ni tsuite no kanketsu na hôkoku - subete no ningen wa, jibun to yarikata ga chigaeba, kore o yaban to iu (A brief report on the damage by loan sharks—If all human beings have a different self and manner, this is called barbaric). Waseda Daigaku Kurejitto Bijinesu Kenkyû-jo Working Papers (Waseda University Institute for Research on Credit Business Working Papers), vol 2

Dworkin R (2002) Sovereign virtue: the theory and practice of equality. Harvard University Press, Cambridge

Economist (2011) Natural disasters: counting the cost. The Economist Online. www.economist.com/blogs/dailychart/2011/03/natural_disasters

Edgington DW (2010) Reconstructing Kobe: the geography of crisis and opportunity. University of British Columbia Press, Vancouver

Feldman EA (2013) Fukushima: catastrophe, compensation, and justice in Japan. DePaul Law Rev 62:335–355

Financial Services Agency (2011a) Kashikin-gyô-hô shikô kisoku no ichibu o kaisei suru naikaku-fu-rei no gaiyô (Outline of the cabinet office ordinance partially amending the ordinance for enforcement of the money lending business law). Financial Services Agency. http://www.fsa.go.jp/news/22/kinyu/20110428-8/01.html

Financial Services Agency (2011b) Press conference by Shozaburo Jimi, Minister for Financial Services (Excerpt. Friday, May 6, 2011, from 12:07 p.m. to 12:31 p.m.). Financial Services Agency. http://www.fsa.go.jp/en/conference/minister/2011/20110506.html

Financial Services Agency (2011c) Press conference by Shozaburo Jimi, Minister for Financial Services (Excerpt. Friday, June 10, 2011, from 9:40 a.m. to 10:08 a.m.). Financial Services Agency. http://www.fsa.go.jp/en/conference/minister/2011/20110610.html

Financial Services Agency (2011d) Tajû saimu sôdan ni kakaru higashi-nihon dai-shinsai e no taiô ni tsuite (About the response to the Great East Japan Earthquake related to multiple debt consultation). Financial Services Agency. http://www.fsa.go.jp/ordinary/earthquake201103/20110421-1.html

Flynn F, Taniguchi T (2010) Credit checks may spell end for 3,000 Japanese consumer lenders. Bloomberg. http://www.bloomberg.com/apps/news?pid=newsarchive&sid=awbGXY1YFvKE

Fourie C, Schuppert F, Wallimann-Helmer I (2015) Social equality: on what it means to be equals. Oxford University Press, Oxford, New York

Gill T, Steger B, Slater DH (eds) (2013a) Japan copes with calamity: ethnographies of the earthquake, tsunami and nuclear disasters of March 2011. Lang, Oxford

Gill T, Steger B, Slater DH (2013b) The 3.11 disasters. In: Gill T, Steger B, Slater DH (eds) Japan copes with calamity: ethnographies of the earthquake, tsunami and nuclear disasters of March 2011, pp 3–23. Lang, Oxford

Godzik M (2013) Rebuilding housing in Japan's tsunami-hit towns and cities. Int J Hous Policy 13:433–445. https://doi.org/10.1080/14616718.2013.852301

Government of Japan, Cabinet Office (2011a) Nihon no saigai taisaku (Disaster management in Japan), Tokyo

Government of Japan, Cabinet Office (2011b) White paper on disaster management 2011 (Executive summary, provisional translation). Government of Japan, Cabinet Office. http://www.bousai.go.jp/kaigirep/hakusho/pdf/WPDM2011_Summary.pdf

Government of Japan, Cabinet Office (2012) White paper on suicide prevention in Japan 2012—digest version. Government of Japan, Cabinet Office. http://www8.cao.go.jp/jisatsutaisaku/whitepaper/en/w-2012/summary.html

Hirayama Y (2000) Collapse and reconstruction: housing recovery policy in Kobe after the Hanshin Great Earthquake. Hous Stud 15(1):111–128

Hirayama Y (2010) The role of home ownership in Japan's aged society. J Hous Built Environ 25(2):175–191

Hirayama Y, Hayakawa K (1995) Home ownership and family wealth in Japan. In: Forrest R, Murie A (eds) Housing and family wealth: comparative international perspectives. Routledge, London, New York, pp 215–230

Hörhager E, Weitzdörfer J (forthcoming) From natural hazard to man-made disaster: the protection of disaster victims in China and Japan. In: Amelung I, Bälz M, Holbig H, Storz C (eds) Protecting the weak: entangled processes of framing, mobilization and institutionalization in East Asia, Routledge, London

Inaba K (2011) Higashi-nihon dai-shinsai to seifu taiô (The Great East Japan Earthquake and the government's reaction). Jurisuto 1427:21–26

Ishibashi H (2014) 89,000 still living in temporary housing in Tohoku disaster area. Asahi Shimbun. http://ajw.asahi.com/article/0311disaster/recovery/AJ201409110032

Iwata M (2007) Social exclusion and homelessness. In Hirayama Y, Ronald R (eds) Housing and social transition in Japan. Housing and society series. Routledge, London, New York, pp 140–164

Iwata M, Nishizawa A (eds) (2008) Poverty and social welfare in Japan (Japanese society series). Trans Pacific Press, Melbourne, Portland, Or

Japan Times (2011) 'Double loan' relief for disaster victims gets nod. The Japan Times. http://www.japantimes.co.jp/news/2011/06/18/national/double-loan-relief-for-disaster-victims-gets-nod/

Japan Times (2012). Double loan problem still a heavy burden for many disaster survivors. The Japan Times. http://www.japantimes.co.jp/news/2012/09/14/business/double-loan-problem-still-a-heavy-burden-for-many-disaster-survivors/

Japan Times (2013) New solutions sought for loan woes. The Japan Times. http://www.japantimes.co.jp/news/2013/09/10/national/new-solutions-sought-for-loan-woes/#.U9zyC9LlrJK
Japan Press Weekly (2011a) Can loan shark money save disaster victims? Japan Press Weekly. http://www.japan-press.co.jp/modules/news/index.php?id=1849
Japan Press Weekly (2011b) JCP urgent proposal to solve disaster victims' 'double loan' problem. Japan Press Weekly. http://www.japan-press.co.jp/modules/news/index.php?id=2088
JFBA (2011a) Bengo-shi hakusho 2011-nen-ban (tokushû 3) Higashi-nihon dai-shinsai ni kan suru nichiben-ren no torikumi - shinsai chokugo o furikaette (White paper on attorneys 2011 (special issue 3) Initiatives of the JFBA related to the Great East Japan Earthquake—Looking back immediately after the earthquake), Tokyo
JFBA (2011b) Double loan problem. JFBA. http://www.nichibenren.or.jp/en/meetings/year/2011/111024.html
JFBA (2011c) Recommendations on relief from unreasonable debt including double loan payments as a result of the Great East Japan Earthquake. JFBA. http://www.nichibenren.or.jp/en/document/opinionpapers/20110422_2.html
JFBA (2011d) White paper on attorneys 2011, Tokyo
JFBA (2012a) Bengo-shi hakusho 2012-nen-ban (tokushû 1) Higashi-nihon dai-shinsai ni kan suru nichiben-ren no hisai-sha shi'en katsudô (White paper on attorneys 2012 (special issue 1) Activities of the JFBA related to the support of victims of the Great East Japan Earthquake), Tokyo
JFBA (2012b) Statement calling for active use of the system for reduction of and exemption from double loan problems for disaster victims (Guidelines for individual debtor out-of-court workouts)—Marking one year since the launch of the system. JFBA. http://www.nichibenren.or.jp/en/document/statements/year/2012/120803_2.html
Johnson C (2007) Strategic planning for post-disaster temporary housing. Disasters 31:435–458 (2007). https://doi.org/10.1111/j.1467-7717.2007.01018.x
Kabashima H (2012) Current issues in legal policy for recovery from the aftermath: one year after the 3.11 Tôhoku Earthquake and Tsunami. J Japan Law 17(34):7–21
Katô N (2012) (Teigen) shinsai fainansu no kakuritsu ni mukete ((Proposal) toward the establishment of [a] natural disaster risk finance system). Shinsai fukkô kenkyû (Stud Disaster Recovery Revital) 4:119–141
Katô T (2013) Great East Japan Earthquake and economic revitalization of enterprises and individuals. By Tetsuo Katô. Waseda University Institute of Comparative Law. http://www.waseda.jp/hiken/en/jalaw_inf/topics2013/topic/001kato.html
Kawamura H (2017) The relation between law and technology in Japan: liability for technology-related mass damage in the cases of minamata disease, asbestos, and the Fukushima Daiichi nuclear disaster. Contemp Jpn 30(1):3–27
Kennedy J, Ashmore J, Babister E, Kelman I (2008) The meaning of 'build back better': evidence from post-tsunami Aceh and Sri Lanka. J Conting Crisis Manag 16(1):24–36
Kingston J (2013) Contemporary Japan: history, politics, and social change since the 1980s, 2nd edn. Wiley, Chichester, West Sussex
Kitamura Y (2011) Kasetsu jûtaku no kyôyo to un'yō (The provision and operation of temporary housing). Jurisuto 1427:46–57
Klein N (2008) The shock doctrine: the rise of disaster capitalism. Metropolitan Books, New York
Kojin saimu-sha no shiteki seiri ni kan suru gaidorain kenkyû-kai [Study group of the guidelines for individual debtor out-of-court workouts] (2011) Kojin saimu-sha no shiteki seiri ni kan suru gaidorain (Guidelines for individual debtor out-of-court workouts). Financial Services Agency. http://www.fsa.go.jp/news/23/20110819-1/01.pdf
Kojin-ban shiteki seiri gaidorain un'ei i'in-kai [Steering committee for the guidelines for individual debtor out-of-court workouts] (2014) Kojin-ban shiteki seiri gaidorain otoiawase kensû-tô (Number of enquiries, etc. on the guidelines for individual debtor out-of-court workouts). Kojin-ban shiteki seiri gaidorain un'ei i'in-kai (Steering committee for the guidelines for individual debtor out-of-court workouts). http://www.kgl.or.jp/kensuu/pdf/kensuu.pdf

Kozuka S (2012) Insurance law issues due to the Great East Japan Earthquake of 2011. J Jpn Law 17(3):33, 34

Kozuka S, Nottage L (2007) Re-regulating unsecured consumer credit in Japan: over-indebted borrowers, the Supreme Court, and new legislation. Sydney Law School Res Pap 07(62):1–30

Krauss E (2013) Crisis management, LDP, and DPJ style. Jpn J Polit Sci 14:177–199. https://doi.org/10.1017/s1468109913000029

Kunreuther H, Pauly M (2004) Neglecting disaster: why don't people insure against large losses? J Risk Uncertain 28(1):5–21

Leflar RB, Hirata A, Murayama M, Ota S (2012) Human flotsam, legal fallout: Japan's tsunami and nuclear meltdown. J Jpn Law 17(34):71–86

Mainichi Daily News (2011) Loan sharks take advantage of financially struggling disaster victims. The Mainichi Daily News. http://mdn.mainichi.jp/mdnnews/national/archive/news/2011/06/18/20110618p2a00m0na002000c.html

Ministry of Internal Affairs and Communications, Statistics Bureau (2013) Statistical handbook of Japan 2013, Tokyo

Murosaki Y (2013) Hanshin awaji dai-shinsai-go no jûtaku saiken to kyojû mondai (Housing reconstruction and residential problems after the Great Hanshin Awaji Earthquake). Saigai Fukkô Kenkyû (Bull Disaster Recovery) 5:107–113

Nihon shihô shi'en senta hôterasu [Japan Legal Support Center Hôterasu] (2013) Higashi-nihon dai-shinsai no hisai-sha-tô e no hôteki shi'en ni kan suru nîzu chôsa hôkoku-sho (Report on the survey on needs of legal assistance to victims, etc. of the Great East Japan Earthquake). Nihon shihô shi'en senta hôterasu (Japan Legal Support Center Hôterasu). http://www.houterasu.or.jp/cont/100526110.pdf

OECD (2013) OECD economic surveys: Japan 2013: special feature: from tragedy to revitalisation, vol 2013. OECD Publishing

Ôgaki H (2013) Shôrai no nijû saimu mondai o ika ni kaihi suru ka - risuku ekusuchenji ichiba no sôsetsu ni mukete (How to avoid double debt problems in the future - towards the creation of a risk-exchange market). Ritsumei-kan hôgaku 349:219–295

Ohira K, Chiba T (2011) Banks grant 10,000 loan deferments to quake victims. Asahi Shimbun. http://www.asahi.com/english/TKY201105190168.html

Okamoto T (2012) Higashi-nihon dai-shinsai hôritsu sôdan kaiseki kekka kara michibiku gyôsei kikan no shin-gyômu keizoku keikaku (Shin-gyôsei BCP) (New business continuity plans of governmental agencies based on the results of [an] analysis of Great East Japan Earthquake legal counseling (New governmental BCP)). Saigai Fukkô Kenkyû (Bull Disaster Recovery) 4:53–65

Okamoto Y, Bretherton J (2012) Homeless people: single men in Japan. In: Smith SJ (ed) International encyclopedia of housing and home. Elsevier, Amsterdam, Oxford, pp 122–126

Ôno K (1996) Jûtaku fukkô ni miru tokuchô to kadai (Characteristics and issues seen in housing recovery). Nihon Fudô-san Gakkai-shi (J Assoc Real Estate Sci) 11(2):26–27

Ranghieri F, Ishiwatari M (2014) Learning from megadisasters: lessons from the Great East Japan Earthquake. World Bank Publications, Washington

Rawls J (1999) A theory of justice. Belknap Press of Harvard University Press, Cambridge, MA

Satake K (2014) The 2011 Tohoku, Japan, earthquake and tsunami. In: Ismail-Zadeh A, Urrutia Fucugauchi J, Kijko A, Takeuchi K, Zaliapin I (eds) Extreme natural hazards, disaster risks and societal implications (Special Publications of the International Union of Geodesy and Geophysics). Cambridge University Press, Cambridge

Shimizu T (2007) The amendment to the money lending law will affect consumer loan securitizations. Asia Law Jpn Rev 2(3):23

Shimizu M (2012) Resilience in disaster management and public policy: a case study of the Tohoku disaster. Risk, Hazards Crisis Public Policy 3:40–59 (2012). https://doi.org/10.1002/rhc3.17

Shûkan Kin'yû Zaisei Jijô (2011) Giron hyakushutsu, nijû saimu mondai no chaku-chiten wa izuko (Often discussed: where is the landing point of the double debt problem?). Shûkan Kin'yû Zaisei Jijô (Financial and Fiscal Situation Weekly) 62(21)(3083):6–7

Steele S, Jin C (2012) Insolvency law responses to a national crisis: Great East Japan Earthquake and guidelines for individual debtor out-of-court workouts. J Jpn Law 17(34):43–70

Temkin LS (1993) Inequality. Oxford University Press, New York, Oxford

Torihata Y (2012) Shinsai fukkô to nijû saimu mondai (Earthquake recovery and the double debt problem). Shizuoka daigaku keizai kenkyû (Shizuoka Univ Econ Rev) 16(4):195–213

Tsukui S (2011) Q&A Hisai-sha seikatsu saiken shi'en-hô (Questions and answers: the act on support for reconstructing livelihoods of disaster victims). Shôji Hômu, Tokyo

Uchida H, Uesugi I, Ono A, Hosono K, Miyazawa D (2012) Keizai-gaku-teki shiten kara mita nijû saimu mondai - kigyô no mondai o chûshin ni (The 'overlapping debt problem' from an economics point of view: centered around the problem for firms). Kin'yû Keizai Kenkyû (Rev Monet Financ Stud) 34:1–27

Ueda Y, Shaw R (2014) Issues and challenges in temporary housing in post-3.11 Kesennuma. In: Shaw R (ed) Community practices for disaster risk reduction in Japan, Disaster Risk Reduction. Springer Japan, Tokyo, pp 209–226

Umeda S (2013) Japan: legal responses to the Great East Japan Earthquake of 2011. By Sayuri Umeda, Foreign law specialist. The Law Library of Congress, Global Legal Research Center. http://www.loc.gov/law/help/japan-earthquake/Great-East-Japan-Earthquake.pdf

Verchick RM (2012) Disaster justice: the geography of human capability. Duke Environ Law Policy Forum 23(23):23–71

Wakabayashi D, Hayashi Y, Fairclough G, Inagaki K, Dvorak P (2011) Japan's way back. Wallstr J. http://online.wsj.com/news/articles/SB10001424053111904900904576554532325467622

Waldenberger F (2013) Confronting earthquake risk in Japan: are private households underinsured? Asia Eur J 11:79–91 (2013). https://doi.org/10.1007/s10308-013-0345-7

Weitzdörfer J (2014) Liability for nuclear damages under Japanese law: key legal problems arising from the Fukushima Daiichi nuclear accident. In: Butt S, Nasu H, Nottage L (eds) Asia-pacific disaster management: comparative and socio-legal perspectives. Springer, Berlin Heidelberg, pp 119–138

Weitzdörfer J (forthcoming) Verbraucherkreditregulierung in Japan (Consumer Credit Regulation in Japan). Mohr Siebeck, Tübingen

Weitzdörfer J, Beard S (forthcoming 2020) Disaster, law and social justice in Japan: the tsunami of debt and lost homes, vol 20. Deutsches Institut für Japanstudien Miscellanea/Iudicium, Vienna, Tokyo

Wilhelm J, Delaney A (2013) No homes, no boats, no rafts: Miyagi coastal people in the aftermath of disaster. In: Gill T, Steger B, Slater DH (eds) Japan copes with calamity: ethnographies of the earthquake, tsunami and nuclear disasters of March 2011. Lang, Oxford, pp 99–124

Williams S, Jacobs K (2011) Disasters, housing, actuarialism and the securitisation of Risk. Hous Stud 26(2):185–195

Yagi T (2007) Hisai-sha no seikatsu saiken shi'en o meguru rongi to rippo no kei'i (Discussions and legislative process of the support for reconstructing livelihoods of disaster victims). Rifarensu (Reference) 11:2–48

Yamamoto T (2011) Dai-kibo saigai to hoken (Insurance and a large-scale disaster). Jurisuto 1427:72–78

Yamanome A (2012) Legal issues on civil matters concerned with [the] great Tohoku earthquake. By Akio Yamanome. Waseda University Institute of Comparative Law. http://www.waseda.jp/hiken/en/jalaw_inf/topics2011/009yamanome.html

Yamasaki E (2003) Hisai-sha seikatsu saiken shi'en-hô no mina'oshi (Reexamination of [the] act [on] support for reconstructing livelihoods of disaster victims). In: Chi'iki Anzen Gakkai Kôgai-shû (Proceedings of the annual conference of the institute of social safety science), vol 13, pp 91–94

Chapter 5
How the Capital Market Reacted to the Great East Japan Earthquake: A Risk Perspective

Soichiro Moridaira

Abstract This chapter studies how the Japanese stock market reacted to the Great East Japan Earthquake. The Nikkei 225 stock index did not show much declining due to the Earthquake compared with the Great Financial crisis of 2007-2008. However, it can be shown that the impact of the Great Earthquake was bigger than that of the Great Financial crisis from the viewpoint of the default (insolvency) probability which may be computed from the stock prices. We furthermore try to show that the impacts of the Great Earthquake upon the stock prices of electric power and insurance companies using the state-space model. We find that the systematic risk representing by stochastically time-varying betas in these firms drastically changed after the Great Earthquake. The betas of all of the electric power companies depending upon the atomic showed strong jump just after the day of the Fukushima power plant collapse resulting from the Great Earthquake. In contrast to this, the betas of the insurers declined reflecting "gain from the loss (Shelor et al. in J Risk Insur 476–488, 1992)."

1 Introduction

Japan is a disaster archipelago exposed to the risk of earthquakes, tsunamis, volcanic eruptions, and largescale wind and flood damage. The Great East Japan Earthquake that happened March 11, 2011 is still fresh in my mind. Also, the Great Hanshin-Awaji Earthquake which occurred on January 17, 1995, is still remembered by many. Reflecting this acute sense of risk, on February 23, 2005, Professor Katsuhiko Ishibashi appeared before the lower house Budget Committee and made the following statement:

> [M]ost seismologists agree that almost the entire Japanese archipelago is entering an active period for large earthquakes. In other words, this highly complex and advanced society will be directly hit by the largest earthquake in the history of mankind. And it will not only be just one. There will be several large earthquake attacks. As a result, without exaggeration,

S. Moridaira (✉)
Emeritus Professor, Keio University, Tokyo, Japan
e-mail: moridaira@waseda.jp

A. Kamesaka and F. Waldenberger (eds.), *Governance, Risk and Financial Impact of Mega Disasters*, Economics, Law, and Institutions in Asia Pacific,
https://doi.org/10.1007/978-981-13-9005-0_5

there is a very high possibility of an earthquake disaster that mankind has not yet seen or experienced.

Large natural disasters cause losses of life and the destruction of houses and vital infrastructures. Beyond this direct damage, they also hit the economy. In the following chapter, I wish to consider the impact of the Great East Japan Earthquake by analyzing how the Japanese capital market, specifically the Tokyo Stock Exchange, reacted to the disaster.

2 Disasters and the National Economy: Not Such a Great Impact?

Many studies have been conducted on the impact of natural disasters on the national economy. The conclusion is that the impact is not so great. For example, Noy (2009) conducted an international comparison, and insists that if the level of the social economic system (literacy rate, per capita income, economic openness, institutional enhancement, government expenditure size, financial strength) is high, the economic impact of an earthquake disaster is not significant even in developing countries. Through similar studies, Cavallo et al. (2013) confirm that the long-term economic impact of disasters is rare unless it causes social anxiety leading to a revolution.

Let us see to what extent this holds true with regard to the economic impact of the Great East Japan Earthquake. Figure 1 shows the daily stock price trend of the long-term Nikkei Average from 2001 to 2016, spanning from before to after the Great East

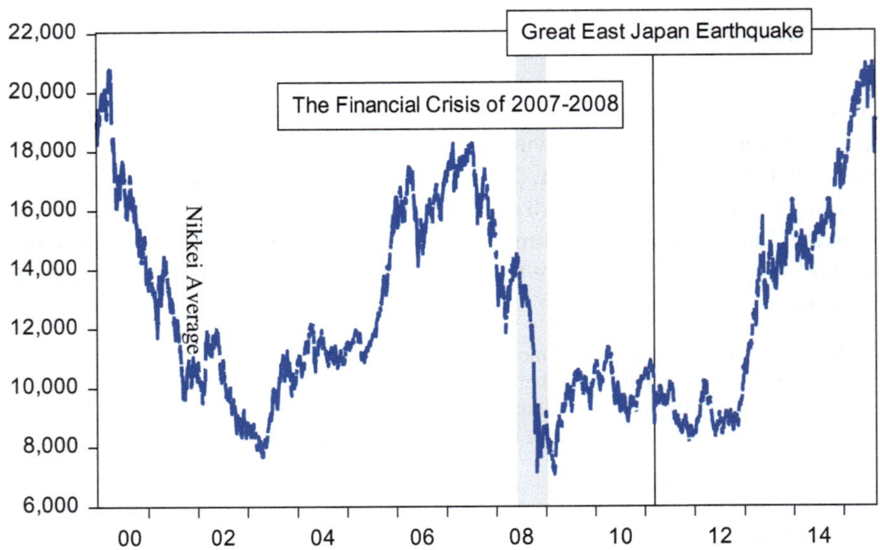

Fig. 1 The impact of the financial crisis and the Great East Japan earthquake on the Nikkei average, Jan 4, 2000–Aug 31, 2015 calendar year

Japan Earthquake. Looking at this, we can see that the Great East Japan Earthquake did not have that great of an impact. Without confirming the date on the horizontal axis, one will not be able to detect the earthquake by looking at the movement of the NIKKEI average. In contrast, the date and time of the financial crisis of 2007–2008 is immediately noticeable. After peaking at 10,044 yen in late June 2006, the Nikkei average dropped to half of that at the end of October, and remained flat for the following six years. In contrast to the 2007–2008 financial crisis, the stock price movements depicted in Fig. 1 clearly support the claims of Noy (2009) and Cavallo et al. (2013) about the economic impact of disasters in the case of the Great East Japan Earthquake.

3 Impact of the Great East Japan Earthquake from the Credit Risk Perspective

Let us look at the credit risk instead of the level of stock prices. Figure 2 shows simple averages of the "probability of insolvency after one year" of companies listed on the TSE for the same period as in Fig. 1.[1] Figure 2 indicates that the probability of insolvency of listed companies was greater at the time when the Great East

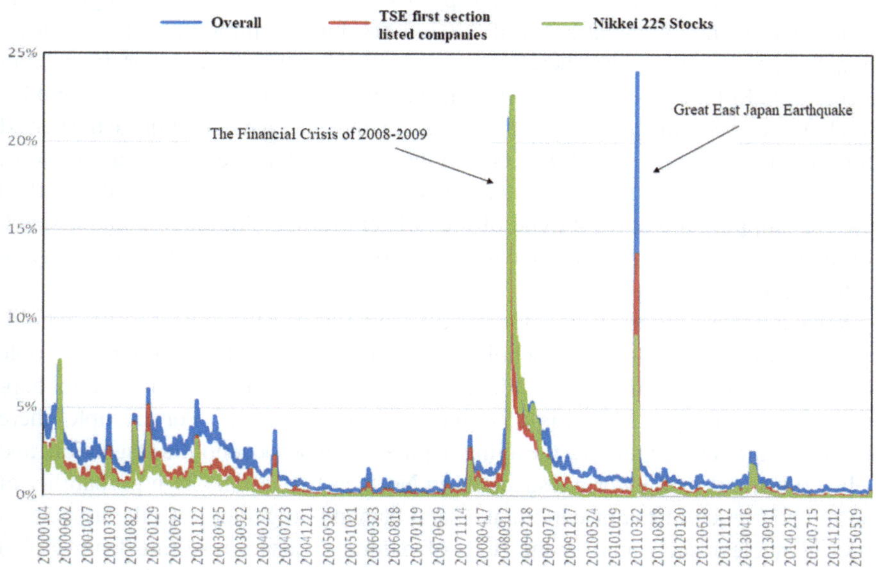

Fig. 2 Default (insolvency) probability trend of listed companies, Jan 4, 2000–Aug 31, 2011

[1]The probability of insolvency (asset value falling below the liability value) of a company after one year can be calculated from the listed company's stock price and its debt value. Details on the calculation and estimation of probability insolvency are explained by Moridaira (2009, 2011).

Japan Earthquake occurred than at the time of the financial crisis of 2007–2008. This finding is quite different from the one derived by considering at the Nikkei Stock average, which suggested that there was no major impact from the Great East Japan Earthquake. We can also see that the impact on the credit risk assessment is smaller for larger companies. The largest companies, which are included in the NIKKEI 225 index experienced a significantly lower increase than the next group of large companies comprising all those listed in the first segment of the Tokyo Stock Exchange. The impact is strongest when considering all listed companies, including the smaller ones listed in other segments.

Figure 2 reveals another important point. From the credit risk perspective and looking at all listed companies, the Great East Japan Earthquake had a greater impact than the financial crisis of 2007–2008. However, the "length" of the impact was much shorter than under the financial crisis.

We have to keep in mind that economic data only capture one part of the story. In the Great East Japan Earthquake, the number of dead or missing amounted to almost 20,000. Also, important household assets, mainly houses, were lost. On the other hand, the financial crisis of 2007–2008 did not kill people or destroy houses. This is of course not reflected in the movement of stock prices. In addition, after the temporary psychological shock of the Great East Japan Earthquake, stock markets may have considered the positive effects of economic stimulus measures resulting from reconstruction demands and huge fiscal expenditures.

After the earthquake, the corporate probability of insolvency was higher than at the time of the Financial crisis of 2007–2008, but it returned to a normal level in approximately a month. Therefore, can we say that there was no problem? Not necessarily. Refer again to Fig. 1. After the Great East Japan Earthquake, the Nikkei Stock Average continued to stagnate, however on the other hand, looking at the period from the financial crisis of 2007–2008 to the great earthquake, an upward trend of the Nikkei Stock Average can be seen. In other words, the great earthquake worked towards stopping the upward trend of the Nikkei average. Although a major shock was avoided, we must acknowledge that the impact of the great earthquake left great "aftereffects."

What are these "aftereffects"? One effect can be seen in the increased "cash holdings." Besides corporations, households hold a large amount of cash in Japan. People were called upon to shift "cash holdings to investments," however, this did not happen. I believe a major reason is a "vague sense of insecurity." For example, there are insecurities accompanying the aging population, macroeconomic stagnation, and political turmoil in the world, especially in Northeast Asia. The high probability of the re-occurrence of major earthquakes and tsunamis together with the associated risks of nuclear accidents, or the risks of natural disasters resulting from global climate change further contributed to this sense of insecurity. Households and corporations alike are considering cash as a financial buffer in times of crisis. Instead of undertaking risky investments in the stock market, corporations and households are considering cash holdings that provide high liquidity as their first choice.

Back in the 1980s, when I was a doctoral student in business school, I was surprised that many professors in finance classes used the phrase, "Cash is King, Cash-flow is

Queen" (cash comes first, cash-flow comes next in importance). Now in Japan, not only corporations, but households also think this way. In other words, there may not be anything as reliable as cash, especially given the extremely low interest and inflation rates. Stocks are risky, investments in government bonds guarantee a fixed nominal return, but they are subject to price risks, and insurance is expensive; therefore, that leaves only cash. This is an issue that everyone concerned about personal finance must consider. In that sense, I believe that the Great East Japan Earthquake and the subsequent nuclear accident continues to exert a great long-term influence.

4 Impact of the Great East Japan Earthquake from the Market Risk Perspective: The Case of Electric Power Companies[2]

Above we have considered the impact of a great earthquake using the credit risk indicator with regard to the probability of insolvency, but now let us consider the impact using the market risk measure. The market risk of individual companies can be measured by the volatility of the stock investment return, which shows the rate of change in stock prices. However, from a finance theory perspective, the correct method is to compare it with the average market volatility, thus taking a relative measure of an individual company's stock volatility.

The stock beta can be depicted by plotting the market average return on investment (ROI) on the horizontal axis, for example the TOPIX ROI, and the individual company's ROI on the vertical axis, for example the ROI of TEPCO. Beta represents the slope of the trend line in the scatter diagram as in Fig. 4. This slope can be expressed as a linear equation. The Eqs. (1) and (2) define the market risk beta in theoretical terms (Eq. 1), and for the empirical estimation (Eq. 2).[3]

$$\text{One factor model } \tilde{\boldsymbol{r}}_t = \boldsymbol{\alpha} + \boldsymbol{\beta r}_{m,t} + \tilde{\boldsymbol{e}}_t \tag{1}$$

$$\text{Linear equation} \quad Y = a + bX + \text{ error} \tag{2}$$

The left side r_t of Eq. (1) represents the stock investment return on day t of the individual company, for example TEPCO; $r_{m,t}$ on the right side shows the stock investment return on day t for a market index, TOPIX in our case. The e_t represents the remaining change in the rate of return not explained by variations in $r_{m,t}$.

[2]Total risk is the sum of undiversifiable risk (systematic risk) and diversifiable risk (unsystematic risk). This chapter considers the impact of the Great East Japan Earthquake on the former. In contrast, empirical analysis of finance and accounting traditionally focused on the impact of an event, such as a disaster, on the latter for such research, refer to Yoshida (2003), Yanase (2014)

[3]To be precise, the rate of return on both sides of Formula (1) uses the excess return defined as that with subtracted risk-free rate. Therefore, the constant term α should be zero in a world where a market equilibrium exists, in short where CAPM holds true.

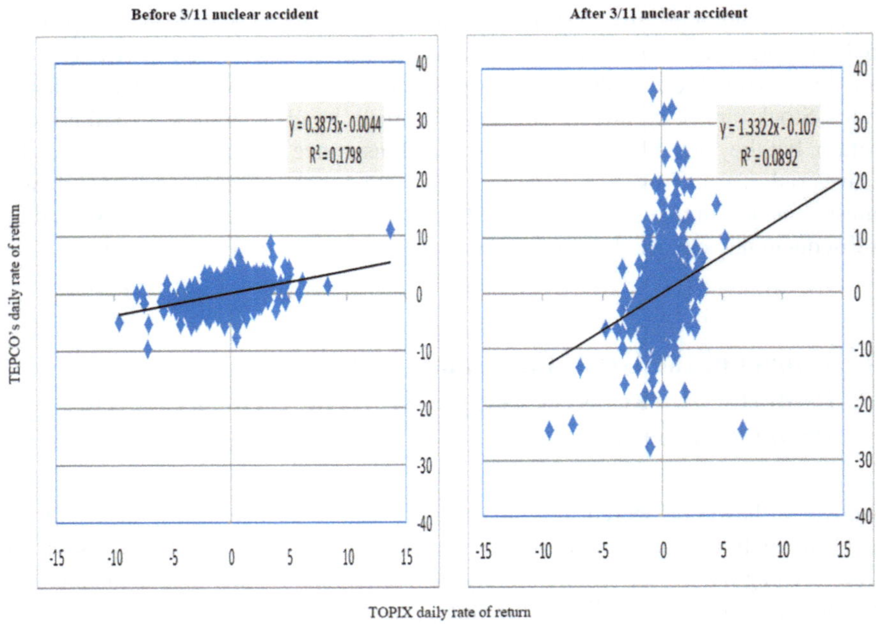

Fig. 3 Market risk beta for TEPCO stock, Apr 2, 2010–Dec 30, 2011. *Note* After the earthquake, TEPCO's beta, the slope of the line, increased by approximately 3.4 times. The rate of return of TOPIX and TEPCO are computed based on the TOPIX index and Stock Price of TEPCO. Index and price data are available from the Nikkei NEEDS database

The results of the empirical estimation are shown in Fig. 3. The estimated variable a on the right side is the Y intercept, and b represents the slope of the line. Because β in Eq. (1) represents the slope of the line, it shows the "sensitivity," the percentage of change to individual stock prices (return on investment) when there is a 1% change in the TOPIX index (ROI). Let us consider their meanings using real figures.

When beta is 1, the stock price is directly proportional to TOPIX, that is, it indicates the same exact movement. Therefore, investors who own such stocks have the same risk and return as investing in the market average, TOPIX. If beta is greater than 1, it means that there is a price fluctuation risk that is larger than the market average. Conversely, if beta is less than 1, the price fluctuation risk is lower than the TOPIX. If the individual stock price does not correlate with the market risk, beta will be zero. An individual stock which is negatively correlated with the market return ($\beta < 0$) will offer insurance against market fluctuations. The above explanation is summarized in Table 1.

The left side of Fig. 3 shows the relationship "before" the earthquake. The slope of the line is small. In fact, "before" the earthquake we obtain the following estimated Eq. (3),

$$\tilde{r}_t = -\mathbf{0.0044} + \mathbf{0.3873}\ r_{m,t} \tag{3}$$

The estimated value for beta is 0.3873, which means that TEPCO's stock will remain at a 0.3873% increase (decrease) even when TOPIX's ROI increases (decreases) by 1%. In other words, the systematic risk of TEPCO's stock is 1/3 that of TOPIX, the market average.

On the other hand, "after" the earthquake the estimated equation changes to.

$$\tilde{r}_t = \mathbf{-0.1070 + 1.3322}\,\boldsymbol{r_{m,t}} \quad (4)$$

The slope of the line increased from 0.3873 to 1.3322, in fact, it rose 3.34 times. In short, TEPCO's systematic risk increased dramatically. Before the earthquake, TEPCO was an attractive stock with low risk and stable dividend payments; however, after the earthquake, it turned and fell into a high-risk, low-return stock. In finance theory, if beta risk, that is, the systematic risk, is greater, the expected return must also be high. This is the meaning of the famous CAPM (capital asset pricing model). Since the risk has increased 3.43 times, expected return must also increase. However, considering the damages following the earthquake and the nuclear power plant decommissioning issue, this was considered impossible. Consequently, the stock prices plummeted.

4.1 Analysis by Stochastic Beta Under State Space Model

The TEPCO beta shown in Fig. 3 was estimated by a statistical method called linear regression analysis. Therefore, only one fixed beta value can be obtained in the sample period used for calculation. On the other hand, it is possible to estimate the beta value with the perspective of beta varying stochastically over time by applying the framework of the State Space Modeling (SSM). SSM uses a statistical method called the Kalman filter.[4] The model consists of the following two equations:

$$\text{Observation equation: } \tilde{\mathbf{r}}_{\mathbf{t}} = \boldsymbol{\alpha} + \tilde{\boldsymbol{\beta}}_{\mathbf{t}}\mathbf{r}_{\mathbf{m,t}} + \tilde{\mathbf{e}}_{\mathbf{t}} \quad (5)$$

Table 1 The meaning of beta, the scale for systematic risk

$\beta = 1$	Completely coordinated with the TSE stock index (market average). Average risk
$\beta > 1$	Value change is larger than TSE stock index (market average). High risk
$\beta < 1$	Value change is smaller than TSE stock index (market average). Low risk
$\beta = 0$	No correlation with TSE stock index (market average). Zero risk
$\beta < 0$	TSE stock index (market average) and value movements are opposite. Negative risk (insurance role)

[4]For an introductory explanation of the Kalman Filter, refer to Commandeur and Koopman (2007).

$$\text{State equation: } \tilde{\boldsymbol{\beta}}_t = \boldsymbol{a}\left(\boldsymbol{b} - \tilde{\boldsymbol{\beta}}_{t-1}\right) + \tilde{\boldsymbol{\varepsilon}}_t \tag{6}$$

where $\tilde{\beta}_t$ is the stochastic (probability) beta at time t, the constant "b" in Eq. (6) is the long run mean of the stochastic beta, the constant "a" in Eq. (6) is the mean reversion coefficient which shows the speed or power of the tendency to return the long-run mean of the beta, and $\tilde{\varepsilon}_t$ is the error term for the state equation. It is assumed that the mean of $\tilde{\varepsilon}_t$ is zero and the variance of it is constant. We also assume that the long-run mean "a" takes values between 0 and 1 so that the stochastic beta does not "explode." Equation (5), which is called an observation (signal) equation, is the same as Eq. (1) except now the beta has subscript t and is a stochastic variable. That is, the beta changes stochastically with time t. We assume that the behavior of beta follows the mean reverting trend shown in Eq. (6). Parameter "a" and "b" in Eq. (6) are estimated by the Maximum Likelihood Method, and the stochastic betas $\tilde{\beta}_t$ in Eqs. (5) and (6) are estimated by the Kalman filtering method. It is possible to estimate three different types of stochastic betas using the Kalman filter, i.e., one-period forecasted, filtered, and smoothed betas. We estimated the smoothed beta using all data in the sample. We only present the smoothed betas in the following Figures. The purpose is to show empirically how the riskiness of stock prices of the electric power companies changed when the East Japan Great Earthquake and the Fukushima Daiichi Nuclear Accident occurred. Our purpose is not to predict the betas.

The estimation results are shown in Fig. 4.[5] After the earthquake, not only did the mean value of the stochastic beta rise, but the fluctuation range (variance) also increased significantly. In other words, the risk of risk measure beta increased.

Figure 5 depicts the transition of the stochastic beta of the four major electric power companies besides TEPCO. We can point out a few interesting observations. Firstly, the stochastic beta of Tohoku Electric Power shows the same movement as in the case of TEPCO. Tohoku Electric Power has a nuclear power plant in Miyagi Prefecture, close to Fukushima. The plant did not experience damages as severe as the ones TEPCO's plants in Fukushima suffered, however the geographic proximity may have somehow induced investors to change their risk assessment similarly.

Secondly, the stochastic beta of Chubu Electric Power and Kansai Electric Power have displayed a larger volatility since the Great East Japan Earthquake. While Kansai Electric Power depends heavily on nuclear power, Chubu Electric Power does not, and the nuclear power plants are located apart from each other. However, because the nuclear power plant owned by Chubu Electric Power is located in an area most susceptible to the impact from a great Tokai/Tonankai earthquake that is expected in the near future, investors adjusted their risk assessment of the two companies in a similar way.

Thirdly, let us look at the case of Kyushu Electric Power. Kyushu Electric Power's stochastic beta came to stay at 1 which was the upper limit of the 95th percentile value of stochastic beta prior to the Great East Japan Earthquake. In other words, as the stochastic beta average rose from 0.3 to 1, its uncertainty became practically zero. Systematic risk stabilized.

[5]For a more detailed analysis, refer to Moridaira (2014).

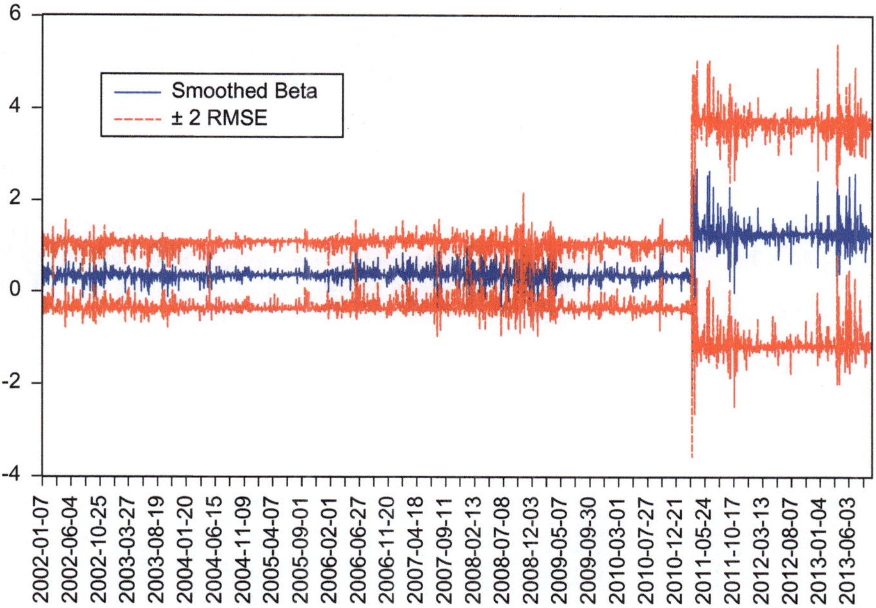

Fig. 4 TEPCO's stochastic betas $\tilde{\boldsymbol{\beta}}_t$ with 95% confidence intervals, Jan 7, 2002–Dec 30, 2011. *Note* 1 Horizontal axis represents business days, vertical axis represents the smoothed stochastic beta value estimated by the Kalman filter. The middle line shows the transition of the mean value of the stochastic smoothed beta. In addition, the lower and the upper lines show the 95% confidence interval ($\pm 2 \times$ Root Mean Squared Error). *Note* 2 To estimate the stochastic beta, the rate of return of TOPIX and TEPCO are computed based on the TOPIX index and TEPCO's stock prices including dividends payments. Index and price data are available from the Nikkei NEEDS database

Another interesting example is shown in Fig. 6, the transition of the stochastic beta for Okinawa Electric Power. From this figure, it cannot be determined when the Great East Japan Earthquake occurred. This means that the systemic risk of Okinawa Electric Power was not influenced by the Great East Japan Earthquake and the Fukushima Daiichi Nuclear Accident at all. It would be wrong to conclude that this is because Okinawa is far away from Tohoku. Kyushu Electric Power's stochastic beta showed a remarkable increase following the earthquake, as shown in Fig. 5, and Kyushu is also far away from Tohoku.

Okinawa Electric Power Company is the only company among the 10 electric power companies that does not rely on nuclear power. Instead, most of the power generation depends on petroleum and coal-fired power. Since the nuclear accident, electric companies from around the world raised dependency on coal and oil, but the risk is not included in Okinawa Electric Power's stochastic beta. The data are not presented here, but the stochastic beta of a large gas company, which also does not depend on nuclear power, did not experience a great impact from the earthquake.

These points indicate that the risk of nuclear power plays a major role in the systematic risk of electric power companies, and eventually, has a great impact on the

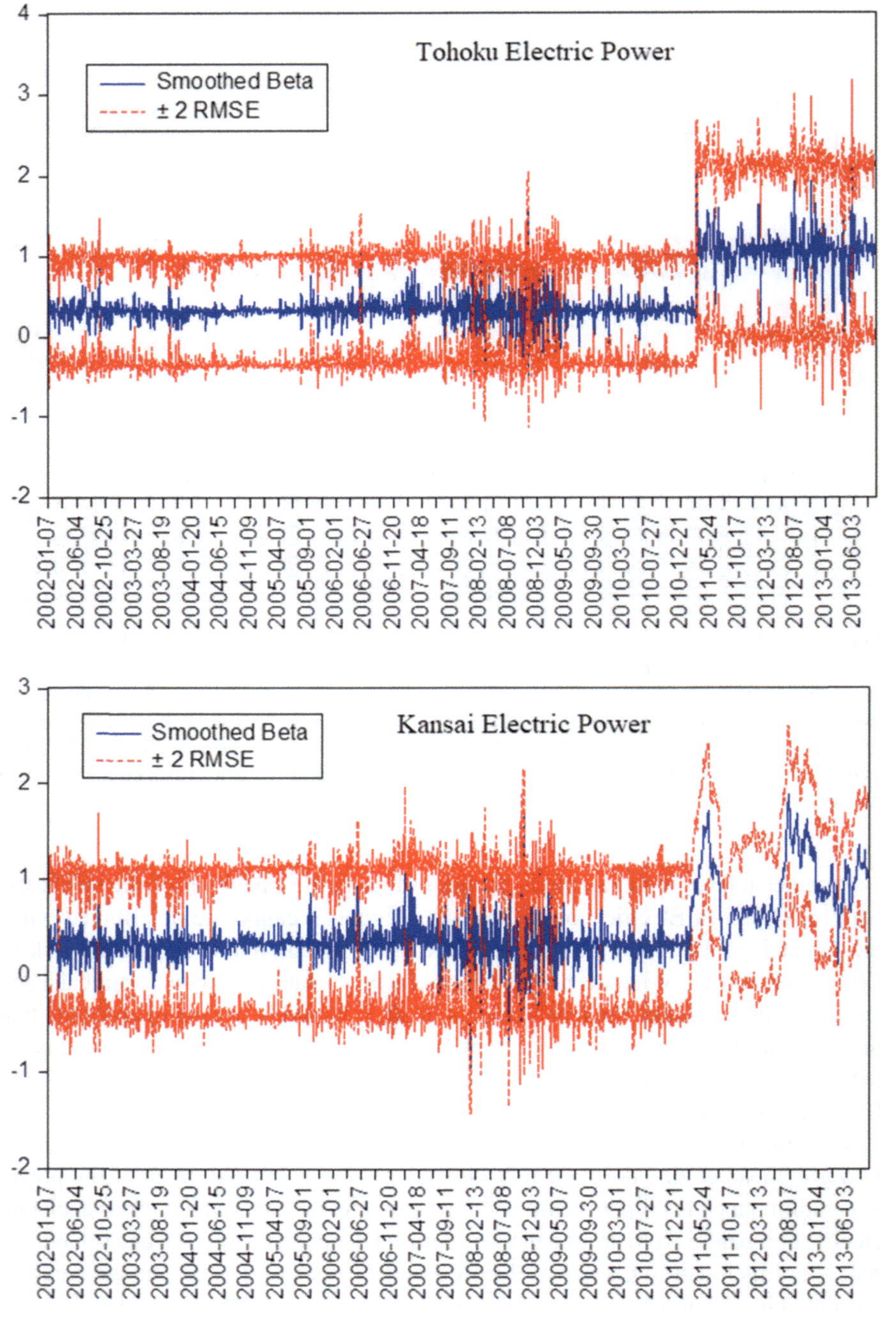

Fig. 5 Transition of four electric power company's stochastic betas $\tilde{\boldsymbol{\beta}}_t$ with 95% confidence intervals, Jan 7, 2002–Dec 30, 2011. *Notes* same as for Fig. 4

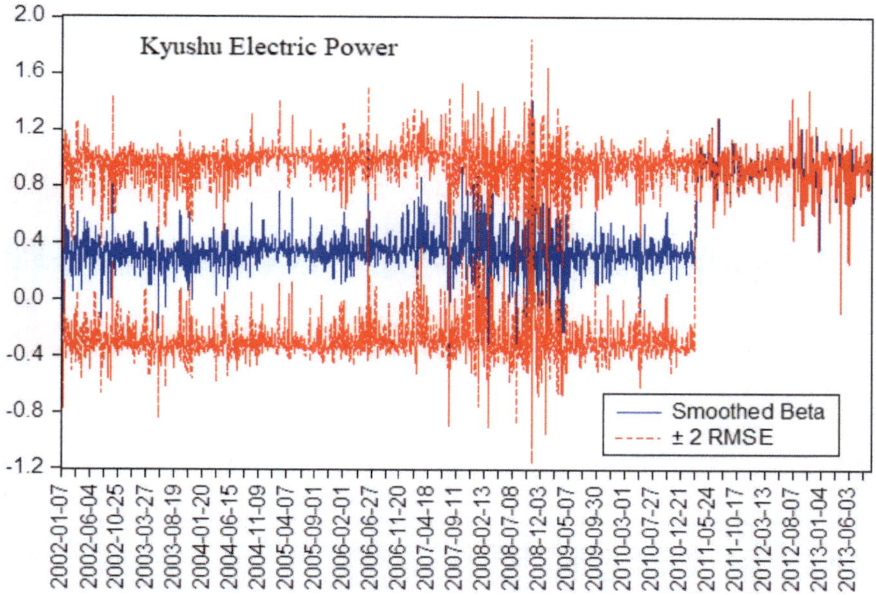

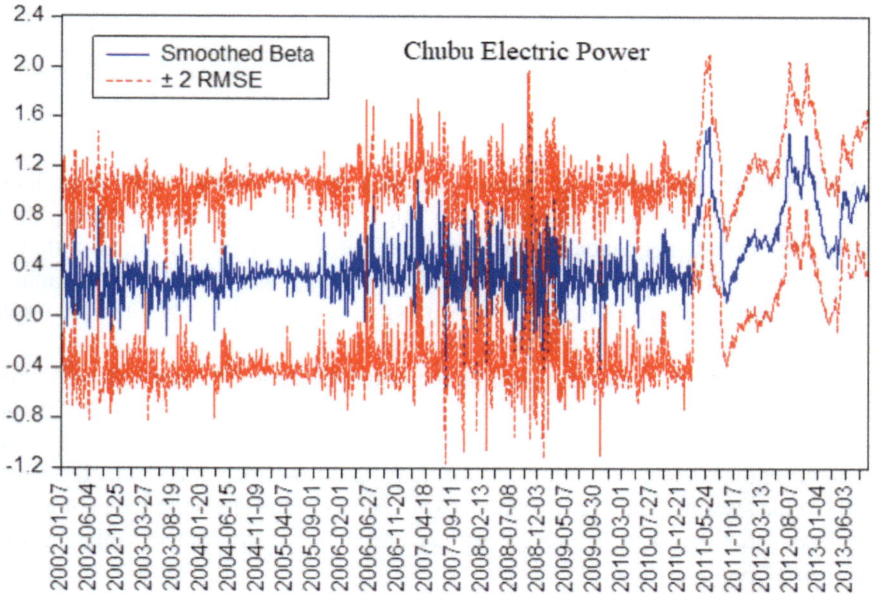

Fig. 5 (continued)

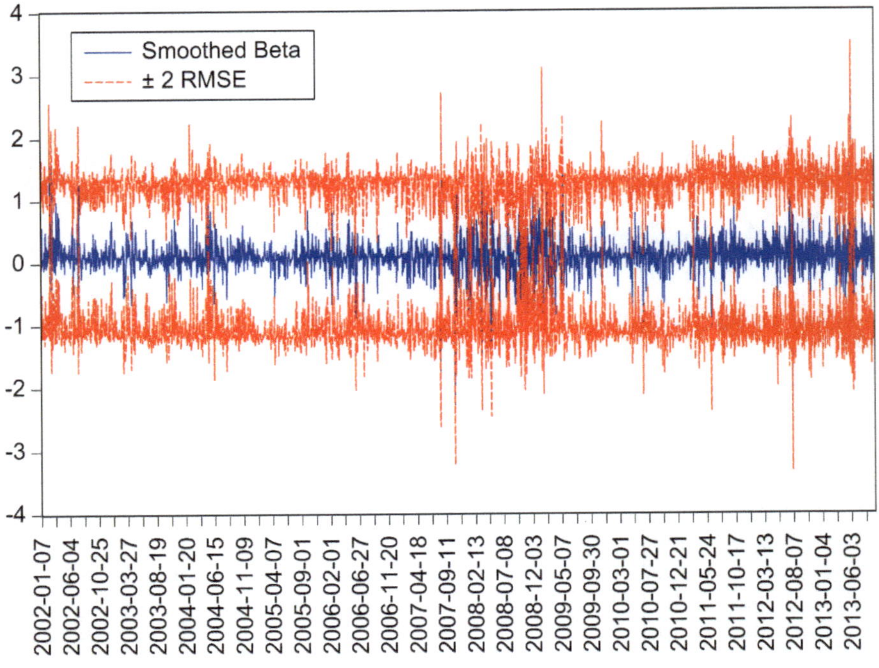

Fig. 6 Okinawa Electric Power Company's stochastic betas $\tilde{\beta}_t$ with 95% confidence intervals, Jan 7, 2002–Dec 30, 2011. *Notes* same as for Fig. 4

expected return demanded by investors. Even from the perspective of the shareholder, who maximizes the corporate value, it is suggested that Japanese electric power companies divest their nuclear power plants. The above analysis suggests that if Japanese electric companies cease to depend on nuclear power plants, their systematic risk will decrease and a there is a high possibility that their corporate value will increase.

This adds further evidence regarding the negative impact of nuclear power companies on the corporate value of power companies. For example, in Kato (2013), the issue of power companies relying on nuclear power is addressed from the perspective of public choice theory. Yet as the present study has also shown, even from the standpoint of the shareholder, who are the ultimate owners of the electric power company, the facts show that dependence on nuclear power by electric power companies is damaging corporate value.

5 Impact of the Great East Japan Earthquake from the Market Risk Perspective: Do Insurance Companies Gain Anything from Disasters?

Disasters will not always negatively affect all companies equally. Certain industries and companies may instead benefit from disasters. Shelor et al. (1992) call this "Gaining from Loss." The construction and real estate industries are typical examples of this. The construction industry TOPIX price index rose sharply in anticipation of reconstruction demands within 15 min after the great earthquake occurred.[6] Stock indexes such as TOPIX were on a declining trend, but since the stock prices of these companies rose, there is a possibility that the beta indicating the relationship between the two could have been negative even for a while.

Another notable example is property insurance companies. If a disaster occurs, the insurance company must make huge payments. Therefore, stock prices of insurance companies should decline and beta should increase. Indeed, the insurance industry showed the biggest drop, minus 3.5%, in the TOPIX stock index on March 11, 2011. However, when considering a longer time span, property insurance companies' beta value instead declined. This is due to the possibility that people who had not considered earthquake risks in the past would rush to buy earthquake insurance policies. If that happens, or if it is anticipated to happen, insurance companies' stock price will increase. In other words, the stock beta of insurance companies may decrease or become negative.

Figure 7 shows the stochastic betas of three major Japanese non-life insurance companies. Clearly after the earthquake, the three mega non-life insurance companies' betas repeat the decline and rise cycle. In the entire period after the earthquake, the average value of the stochastic beta is not much different from the average before the disaster, but there is a period when the beta is significantly lower than before the disaster. There are two reasons for this.

Firstly, the insurance companies had prepared for the disaster risk. In preparation for situations where huge payments are made in a short amount of time in the event of a major disaster, property insurance companies hold large amounts of cash or equivalent assets in the form of "reserves for catastrophes." Although this may have been done at the request of internal risk management, it may also be due to insurance companies having to comply with capital requirement rules. In either case, I believe the capital requirement performed its function to some extent. This is different from the time of the Great Hanshin-Awaji Earthquake, when the stochastic beta of many casualty insurance companies increased instead.

Secondly, the rate setting for Japanese earthquake insurance is "No Loss, No Profits." Earthquake insurance is underwritten by the Japanese government; therefore, even if there are large payments, most of the risk is taken on by the government. In

---

[6] Although the Great East Japan Earthquake occurred at 2:45 pm on March 11, 2011, real estate shares on the TSE showed a considerable increase in the 15 min until the end of trade at 3 o'clock. Real estate share rates increased by 2% on that day.

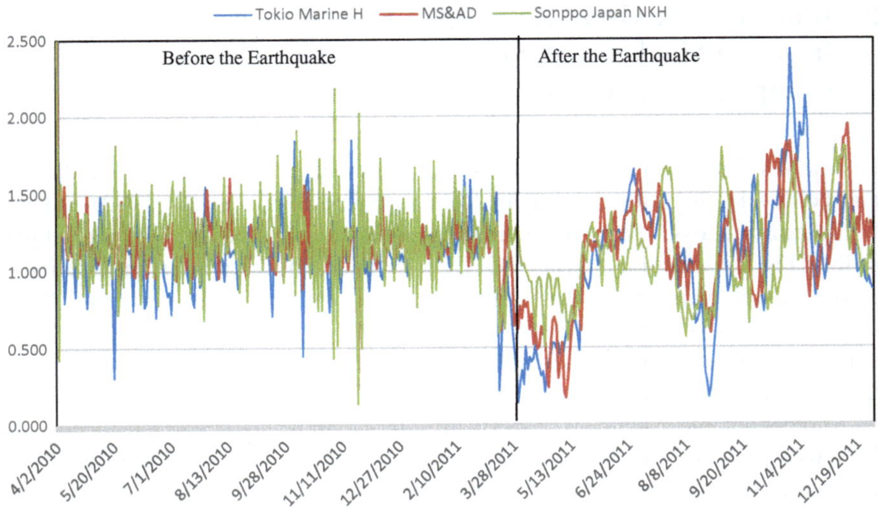

Fig. 7 Smoothed Stochastic Betas $\tilde{\boldsymbol{\beta}}_t$ in Eqs. (**5**) and (6) of three non-life insurance companies before and after the earthquake, Apr 2, 2010–Dec 30, 2011. *Note* The beta increase at the end of August 2011 is believed to be the effect of large aftershocks that occurred during this period. The beta increase from mid-May 2011 is speculated to be due to confirmation of the amount of damage from the earthquake

other words, one of the reasons could be that the risk is widely transferred to the citizens as tax payers, and not borne by the insurance companies.

6 Summary and Conclusion

Using the Great East Japan Earthquake as an example, we analyzed how a huge natural disaster impacted the Japanese stock market, both the market risk and the credit risk.

Our credit risk measure was based on the stock price and corporate debt value and estimated the corporate "insolvency stochastic" by applying option pricing theory. As a result, we could see that smaller companies tended to experience a stronger increase in insolvency risk. When looking at all listed companies, we found that the Great East Japan Earthquake had a stronger impact on credit risk than economic shocks such as the financial crisis. However, compared to the financial crisis, the impact of the earthquake did not last long. Nevertheless, it certainly contributed to a "vague sense of insecurity," leading to higher cash hoarding and thus indirectly reduced investment and growth of the economy.

Regarding the market risk, we analyzed how the probabilistic stock beta of individual companies calculated on a daily basis changed before and after the earthquake.

The companies analyzed were electric power companies and property insurance companies.

In the case of TEPCO, the owner of the Fukushima Daiichi power plant, it was found that the beta, which had been very low before the earthquake increased by 3.4 times as a result of the earthquake and the nuclear disaster. The betas of other major electric power companies examined were similarly affected although to different degrees. The only exception was Okinawa Electric Power which operates no nuclear power plants. The company's stochastic beta and its average value and variance never significantly fluctuated. This supports the conclusion that electric power companies' business risk was less influenced by the risk of rising fuel costs after a nuclear accident, but rather reflects the risk of possible future nuclear accidents.

While insurance companies are at risk of having to pay out huge amounts of insurance claims after an earthquake, the risk indicated by the beta rather declined. This indicates that Japanese insurance companies were temporarily "gaining from loss."

The Japanese islands are said to be a disaster archipelago. Corporations, households, national and local governments must deal with various natural disaster risks such as earthquakes and tsunamis, as well as volcanic eruptions. In addition, there are increasing risks caused by global warming. By analyzing how stocks and bond markets, exchange markets, and commodity markets respond to such natural disasters, we can learn what kind of risk management we should aim for be it in our role as national and local governments, individual investors or profit-maximizing corporations.

References

Cavallo E, Galiani S, Noy I, Pantano J (2013) Catastrophic natural disasters and economic growth. Rev Econ Stat 95(5):1549–1561

Commandeur JJ, Koopman SJ (2007) An introduction to state space time series analysis. Oxford University Press, Oxford

Kato H (2013) Nihon saisei saishû kankoku – genpatsu sokuji zero de mirai o hiraku (Final recommendation for regenerating Japan: creating a future with zero nuclear power). Bijinesu-sha (Business Publishing Company)

Moridaira S (2009) Shin'yô risukumoderingu – sokutei to kanri (ôyô fainansu kôza) (Credit risk modeling: measurement and management). Asakurashoten (Asakura Publishing)

Moridaira S (2011) Shin'yô risuku no sokutei to kanri – ekuseru de manabu moderingu (Measurement and management of credit risk modeling: learning modeling through Excel). Chûôkeizaisha (Chuokeiza-sha Publishing)

Moridaira S (2014) Genpatsu jiko wa denryokukaisha no shisutematikku risuku ni dono-sama ni eikyô shita no ka? – Jôtai kûkan moderu o mochiita ibentosutadi no teian (How the nuclear plant accident affected the electric power company's systematic risk: proposal for event study using state space model). Nihon Fainansu Gakkai Taikai Yokô (Japan Finance Society Convention Preliminary Report)

Noy I (2009) The macroeconomic consequences of disasters. J Dev Econ 88(2):221–231

Shelor RM, Anderson DC, Cross ML (1992) Gaining from loss: property-liability insurer stock values in the aftermath of the 1989 California earthquake. J Risk Insur, 476–488

Yanase N (2014) Jishin to songai hokenkaisha no kabu (Earthquakes and non-life insurance company shares). Songai Hoken Kenkyû (Non-life Insur Res) 75(4):241–251

Yoshida Y (2003) Hanshin daishinsai ni okeru ginkôkabu no densen kôka (Infectious effects on bank stocks of the Great Hanshin Earthquake). Gendai Disukurôjâ Kenkyû (Mod Discl Res) 4(March):43–51

Chapter 6
Systemic Risks: Common Characteristics and Approaches for Improving Resilience

Ortwin Renn

Abstract In this article, I aim to delineate the genesis and analytical scope of risk governance. Risk governance pertains to the various ways in which many actors, individuals and institutions, public and private, deal with risks surrounded by uncertainty, complexity and/or ambiguity. The ambition is that risk governance provides a conceptual as well as normative basis for how to deal responsibly with complex risks. I propose to synthesize the body of scholarly ideas and proposals on the governance of risks in a set of management regimes: the combination of risk-based, precautionary and discourse-based management regimes. This set of regimes should be read as a synthesis of what needs to be seriously considered in organizing structures and processes to govern risks and to include stakeholders in the assessment and evaluation of risks.

1 Introduction

The history of the last four decades has been a success story in terms of conventional risk management. This success of conventional risk management is well documented. Referring to Germany, the number of fatal accidents at work decreased from almost 5,000 in 1960 to less than 400 in 2014; the number of traffic accidents from 22,000 in 1972 to 3,700 in 2014; the number of fatal heart attacks and strokes decreased from 109 cases per 100,000 to 62 in the time period between 1992 and 2002 (Renn 2014). In addition, the number of chronic illnesses as well as fatal diseases from environmental pollution or accidents has steadily declined over the past three decades.

Conventional risks in terms of accidents and most illnesses have been successfully reduced (Renn 2015). A fire, for example, may destroy a school, which could lead to

O. Renn (✉)
Institute for Advanced Sustainability Studies (IASS), Potsdam, Germany
e-mail: Ortwin.renn@iass-potsdam.de

Chair of Environmental Sociology and Technology Assessment, University of Stuttgart, Stuttgart, Germany

A. Kamesaka and F. Waldenberger (eds.), *Governance, Risk and Financial Impact of Mega Disasters*, Economics, Law, and Institutions in Asia Pacific,
https://doi.org/10.1007/978-981-13-9005-0_6

the direct loss of the facility, and to the interruption of the affected children's education. However, in an age when fires are prevented from consuming entire cities, the impact of almost any blaze is likely to be limited. When fire breaks out at a school, safety equipment, sprinklers, and routine fire drills (some of the basic tools of conventional risk management) are likely to be effective. With appropriate safeguards in place, the odds are minimal that lives will be lost, or even that anyone will suffer serious physical harm. What is more, the economic cost is almost certain to be limited by insurance claims and contingency budgets, while disaster planning probably means that the lives of teachers and students are disrupted for no more than a few days.

The picture becomes less favorable, however, if we look at globally interconnected, non-linear risks such as those posed, for example, by the global financial system, climate change or the growing inequality between rich and poor. In order to take account of this situation, the Organization for Economic Co-operation and Development (OECD) introduced the new category of 'systemic risk' (OECD 2003). A widely-used definition of a systemic risk was provided by Kaufman and Scott (2003). While they defined systemic risks in the context of financial systems, their definition accommodates much broader systems, like the global climate. "Systemic risk refers to the risk or probability of breakdowns in an entire system, as opposed to breakdowns in individual parts or components, and is evidenced by co-movements (correlation) among most or all parts" (Kaufman and Scott 2003, p. 372). This definition is far from being comprehensive and distinctive. If you think of a car as a system of parts, the total breakdown of a car would certainly not qualify as a systemic risk. Likewise, a partial breakdown of the world's finance system may be severe enough to be called a systemic risk, even if the entire system is not affected. Jaeger et al. have therefore suggested to use a more Wittgensteinian approach by specifying the properties that are associated with systemic risks without claiming to have a complete or mutually exhaustive list (Renn et al. 2017). The main thrust of systemic risks is, however clear: systemic risk refers to a potential collapse of a system of critical importance that involves many interacting elements that are poorly understood. This dimension of a large potential threat within a complex web of interacting elements distinguishes systemic risk from other types of risk.

Jaeger et al. include four major properties of systemic risks (Renn 2016): they are (a) transboundary in nature, (b) highly interconnected and intertwined leading to complex causal structures and dynamic evolutions, (c) non-linear in the cause-effect relationships showing often unknown tipping points or tipping areas and (d) stochastic in their effect structure. Systemic risks tend to be underestimated and do not attract the same amount of attention as catastrophic events. The main reasons here include that complex structures defy human intuition based on the assumption that causality is linked to proximity in time and space. However, complexity implies that far-fetched and distant changes can have major impacts on the system under scrutiny. The second reason is that humans tend to learn by trial and error. Facing non-linear systems with tipping points/areas, people are encouraged to repeat their errors because the feedback is positive for a long time. However, if one surpasses the tipping point the error is so dramatic that learning from crisis is either impossible or extremely costly. Thirdly, systemic risks touch upon the well-known common pool problem: each actor contributes only marginally to the systemic risk so there is no incentive to change one's behavior (Renn 2011). Furthermore, every actor wins if he or she takes the free rider position and let all the others invest in reducing the risk, since all will in the end share the benefits. So, there are many reasons for systemic risks to be underestimated or, at least, under-managed compared to conventional risks.

Another key characteristic that sets systemic risks apart from conventional risks is that their negative material impacts (sometimes immediate and obvious, but often subtle and latent) have the potential to trigger severe ripple effects outside of the domain where the risk is located (OECD 2003). When a systemic risk becomes a calamity, the resulting ripple effects can cause a dramatic sequence of secondary and tertiary spin-off impacts (Kasperson et al. 2003). They may be felt in a wide range of seemingly divergent social systems, from the economy to the health system, inflicting harm and damage in domains far beyond their own. A commercial sector, for example, may suffer significant losses as a result of a systemic risk as we witnessed in the financial crisis in the aftermath of the Lehman Brothers collapse. Even fairly healthy financial institutions were negatively affected and, in the end, taxpayers had to pay the bill for the reckless behavior of a few.

Another example is the BSE (Bovine Spongiform Encephalopathy) debacle in the United Kingdom which not only affected the farming industry but also the animal feed industry, the national economy, public health procedures, and politics (Wynne and Dressel 2001). People refused to eat British beef, regardless of the tangible evidence showing little danger to their health or safety.

Systemic risks represent wicked problems as they are difficult to anticipate and define, have no clear solutions and are seemingly intractable, often plagued by chronic policy failures and intense disagreement (Nursimulu 2015). Systemic risks can trigger unexpected large-scale changes of a system or imply uncontrollable large-scale threats to it (Helbing 2010) and may cause ripple effects beyond the domain in which the risks originally appear (Renn 2016). The consequences of failing to appreciate and manage the characteristics of complex global systems and problems can be immense (Helbing 2012).

2 Major Characteristics of Systemic Risks

The concept of systemic risks grasps different risk phenomena as well as economic, social and technological developments and policy-driven actions at the national and international level. Systemic risks entail endangering potentials with wide-ranging, transnational impacts where conventional risk management and national risk regulation are insufficient. Three major components of systemic risks deserve special attention (Klinke and Renn 2002):

- *Complexity*: Complexity refers to the difficulty of identifying and quantifying causal links between a multitude of potential candidates and specific adverse effects. The nature of this difficulty may be traced back to interactive effects among these candidates (synergisms and antagonisms), positive and negative feedback loops, long delay periods between cause and effect, inter-individual variation, intervening variables, and others. It is precisely these complexities that make sophisticated scientific investigations necessary since the dose–effect relationship is neither obvious nor directly observable. Nonlinear response functions may also result from feedback loops that constitute a complex web of intervening variables.
- *Uncertainty*: Uncertainty comprises different and distinct components such as statistical variation, measurement errors, ignorance and indeterminacy (van Asselt 2000). They all have one feature in common: uncertainty reduces the strength of confidence in the estimated cause and effect chain. If complexity cannot be resolved by scientific methods, uncertainty increases. But even simple relationships may be associated with high uncertainty if either the knowledge base is missing or the effect is stochastic by its own nature.
- *Ambiguity*: Ambiguity denotes the variability of (legitimate) interpretations based on identical observations or data assessments. Most of the scientific disputes in risk analysis do not refer to differences in methodology, measurements or dose-response functions, but to the question of what all this means for human health and environmental protection. Emission data is hardly disputed. Most experts debate, however, whether an emission of x constitutes a serious threat to the environment or to human health. Ambiguity may come from differences in interpreting factual statements about the world or from differences in applying normative rules to evaluate a state of the world. In both cases, ambiguity exists on the grounds of differences in criteria or norms to interpret or judge a given situation. An example of such ambiguity is pesticide residues in food where most analysts agree that the risk to human health is extremely low yet many demand strict regulatory actions. High complexity and uncertainty favor the emergence of ambiguity, but there are also quite a few simple and almost certain risks that can cause controversy and thus ambiguity.

Systemic risks also trigger secondary and tertiary consequences regarding time and space, i.e. functional and territorial dimensions of political, social and economic spheres. The cross-border impact of systemic risks exceeds the scope of domestic regulations and state-driven policies. To handle systemic risks interdisciplinary mechanisms in international governance are required (Klinke and Renn 2012).

3 Systemic Risk Evaluation

3.1 Inclusion of Additional Evaluation Criteria

A holistic and comprehensive concept for assessing and managing systemic risks needs to go beyond the two classic components: extent of damage and probability of occurrence. This raises the question: Which other physical and social impact categories should be included in order to cope with the phenomenological challenges of systemic risks and how can one justify the selection?

The German Advisory Council on Global Change (WBGU 2000) has addressed this problem in its 1998 Annual Report. The Council organized several expert surveys on risk criteria (including experts from the social sciences) and performed a meta-analysis of the major insights from risk assessment and perception studies. The Council also consulted the literature on similar approaches in countries such as United Kingdom, Denmark, Netherlands and Switzerland. They asked experts to provide special reports on this issue to the authors. The following criteria were selected as the result of a long exercise of deliberation and investigations:

- Extent of damage: adverse effects in natural units such as deaths, injuries, production losses etc.;
- probability of occurrence: estimate for the relative frequency of a discrete or continuous loss function;
- incertitude: overall indicator for different uncertainty components;
- ubiquity defines the geographic dispersion of potential damages (intragenerational justice);
- persistency defines the temporal extension of potential damages (intergenerational justice);
- reversibility describes the possibility to restore the situation to the state before the damage occurred (possible restoration includes e.g. reforestation and cleaning of water);
- delay effect characterizes a long time of latency between the initial event and the actual impact of damage. The time of latency could be of physical, chemical or biological nature;
- violation of equity describes the discrepancy between those who grasp the benefits and those who bear the risks; and
- potential of mobilization is understood as violation of individual, social or cultural interests and values generating social conflicts and psychological reactions by individuals or groups who feel inflicted by the risk consequences. They could also result from perceived inequities in the distribution of risks and benefits.

After the WBGU proposal had been reviewed and discussed by many experts and risk managers, Klinke and Renn refined the compound criterion "mobilization" and divided it into four major elements (Klinke and Renn 2002):

- Inequity and injustice associated with the distribution of risks and benefits over time, space and social status;

- psychological stress and discomfort associated with the risk or the risk source (as measured by psychometric scales);
- potential for social conflict and mobilization (degree of political or public pressure on risk regulatory agencies);
- spill-over effects that are likely to be expected when highly symbolic losses have repercussions on other fields such as financial markets or loss of credibility in management institutions.

3.2 *Risk Classification: Six Different Risk Classes*

Given the nine criteria and the numerous sub-criteria, a huge number of risk classes can be deduced theoretically. But a huge number of classes would not be useful for the purpose of placing them in a rather simple traffic light model. Considering the task of generating, legitimizing and communicating risk management strategies, risks with one or several extreme qualities need special attention. Such similar risk phenomena are subsumed under one risk class in which they reach or exceed the same extreme qualities.

Events of damages with a probability of almost one were excluded from this classification. High potentials of damages with a probability near one are clearly located in the intolerable area and therefore unacceptable. By the same token, probability heading towards zero is harmless as long as the associated potential of damage is small. Excluded from the analysis were also small-scale accidents with limited damage potential for each individual case that generate a large number of victims due to their ubiquitous occurrence (such as car accidents). Given these specifications and exceptions, the exercise produced six different risk clusters that the WBGU illustrated with Greek mythology. The mythological names were not selected for illustrative purposes only (Klinke and Renn 1999). When studying the Greek mythology of the time between 700 and 500 BC, the Council became aware of the fact that these "stories" reflected the transition from an economy of small subsistence farmers and hunters to an economy of more organized agriculture and animal husbandry. This transition with its dramatic changes implied a new culture of anticipation and foresight. It also marked the transition from a human self-reflection as being an object of nature to becoming a subject to nature. The various mythological figures demonstrate the complex issues associated with the new self-awareness of creating future rather than just being exposed to fate.

Risk Class Sword of Damocles

According to the Greek mythology, Damocles was once invited by his king to a banquet. However, at the table he had to eat his meal under a razor-sharp sword hanging on a fine thread. Chance and risk are tightly linked for Damocles and the Sword of Damocles became a symbol for a threatening danger in luck. The myth does not tell about a snapping of the thread with its fatal consequences. The threat rather

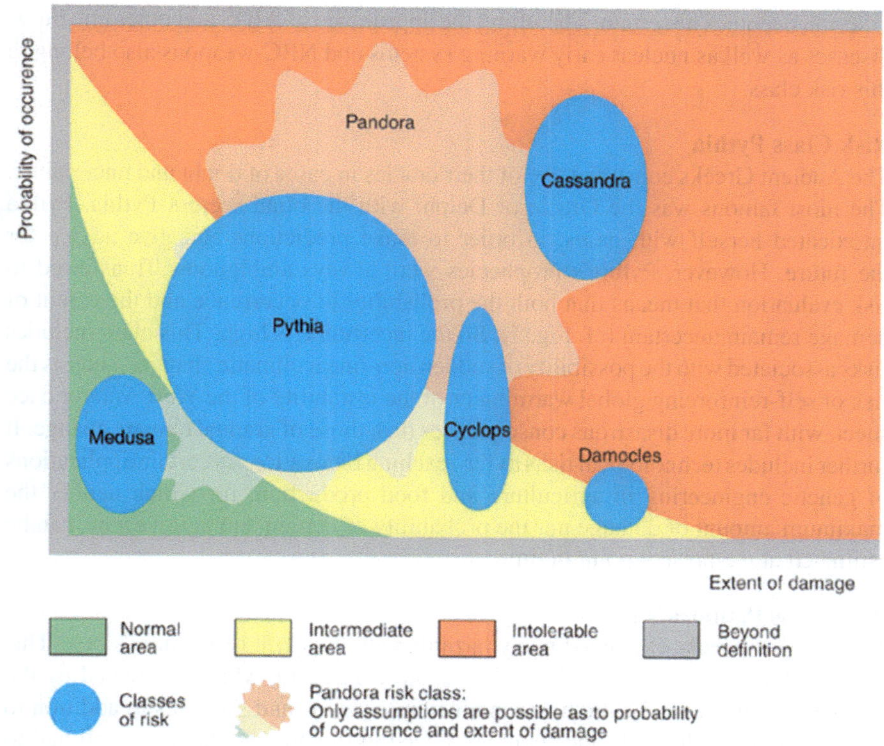

Fig. 1 Risk classes. *Source* WBGU (2000)

comes from the possibility that a fatal event could occur for Damocles any time even if the probability is low. This can be transferred to risks with large damage potentials. Many sources of technological risks have a very high disaster potential, although the probability that this disaster potential manifests itself as a damage is extremely low (cf. Fig. 1). The prime characteristic of this risk class is the combination of low probability with high extent of damage. Typical examples are technological risks such as nuclear energy, large-scale chemical facilities and dams.

Risk Class Cyclops

The Ancient Greeks tell of mighty giants who were punished by only having a single eye, which was why they were called Cyclops. With only one eye, only one side of reality can be perceived and the dimensional perspective is lost. When viewing risks, only one side can be ascertained while the other remains uncertain. Likewise, for risks belonging to the class of Cyclops the probability of occurrence is largely uncertain, whereas the disaster potential is high and relatively well known (cf. Fig. 1). A number of natural hazards such as earthquakes, volcanic eruptions, floods and El Niño belong to this category. There is often too little knowledge about causal factors. In other cases, human behavior influences the probability of occurrence so that this criterion becomes uncertain. Therefore, the appearance of AIDS and other infectious diseases as well as nuclear early warning systems and NBC-weapons also belong to this risk class.

Risk Class Pythia

The Ancient Greeks consulted one of their oracles in cases of doubt and uncertainty. The most famous was the Oracle of Delphi with the blind seeress Pythia. Pythia intoxicated herself with gases, in order to make predictions and give advice for the future. However, Pythia's prophecies were always ambiguous. Transferred to risk evaluation that means that both the probability of occurrence and the extent of damage remain uncertain (cf. Fig. 1). So the incertitude is high. This class includes risks associated with the possibility of sudden non-linear climatic changes, such as the risk of self-reinforcing global warming or of the instability of the West Antarctic ice sheet, with far more disastrous consequences than those of gradual climate change. It further includes technological risks as far-reaching innovations in certain applications of genetic engineering in agriculture and food production, for which neither the maximum amount of damage nor the probability of certain damaging events can be estimated at the present point in time.

Risk Class Pandora's Box

The Ancient Greeks explained many hazards with the myth of Pandora's box. This box was brought down to earth by the beautiful Pandora, who was created by the god Zeus. Unfortunately, the box contained many evils and scourges in addition to hope. As long as the evils and scourges stayed in the box, no damage at all had to be feared. However, when the box was open, all evils and complaints were released and caused irreversible, persistent and wide-ranging damages. A number of human interventions in the environment also cause wide-ranging, persistent and irreversible changes without a clear attribution to specific damages—at least during the time of diffusion. Often these damages are discovered only after the ubiquitous diffusion has occurred.

Risk Class Cassandra

Cassandra, a seeress of the Trojans, predicted correctly the perils of a Greek victory, but her compatriots did not take her seriously. The risk class Cassandra dwells on this paradox: The probability of occurrence as well as the extent of damage are high and relatively well known, but there is a considerable delay between the triggering event and the occurrence of damage. That leads to the situation that such risks are ignored or downplayed. The anthropogenic climate change and the loss of biological diversity are such risk phenomena. Many types of damage occur with high probability, but the delay effect leads to the situation that no one is willing to acknowledge the threat. Of course, risks of the type Cassandra are only interesting if the potential of damage and the probability of occurrence are relatively high. That is why this class is located in the "intolerable" red area (cf. Fig. 1).

Risk Class Medusa

The mythological world of the Ancient Greeks was full of dangers that threaten people, heroes and even Olympic gods. The imaginary Gorgons were particularly terrible. Medusa was one of the three imaginary Gorgon sisters, who the ancient Greeks feared, because her appearance turns the beholder to stone (cf. Fig. 1). Similar to the Gorgons, who spread fear and horror, some new phenomena have a similar effect on modern people. Some innovations are rejected although they are hardly assessed scientifically as a threat, but they have special characteristics that make them individually or socially frightening or unwelcome. Such phenomena have a high potential of psychological distress and social mobilization in public. This risk class is only of interest if there is a particularly large gap between lay risk perceptions and expert risk analysis. A typical example is electromagnetic fields, whose extent of damage was assessed as low by most experts because neither epidemiologically nor toxicologically significant adverse effects could be proven (Wiedermann et al. 2000). Exposure, however, is wide-ranging and many people feel involuntarily affected by this risk.

4 Systemic Risk Management

4.1 Addressing Complexity, Uncertainty and Ambiguity

The essential aim of the risk classification is to judge the acceptability of risk and to design appropriate risk reduction measures if the risk is regarded as intolerable. The six risk types assist risk managers to derive effective and feasible strategies for risk management as well as design regulations and policies.

The characterization provides a knowledge base so that political decision makers have better guidance on how to select measures for each risk class. The strategies pursue the goal of transforming unacceptable into acceptable risks, i.e. the risks should not be reduced to zero but moved into the normal area, in which routine risk management becomes sufficient to ensure safety and integrity.

A comparative view on the risk classification scheme (Table 1) indicates that one can distinguish three central categories of risk management, namely science-based, precautionary and discursive strategies. The two risk classes Damocles and Cyclops require mainly science-based management strategies—more precisely, the Cyclops-risk class requires a combination of risk-based and precautionary strategies—the risk classes Pythia and Pandora demand the application of the precautionary principle, and the risk classes Cassandra and Medusa require discursive strategies for building consciousness, trust and credibility. These three management strategies relate to the main challenges of risk management: complexity, uncertainty and ambiguity.

Understanding and managing complexity, uncertainty and ambiguity is a major task of systemic risk management (Renn and Klinke 2016). As stated above: Complexity refers to the difficulty of identifying and quantifying causal links between a multitude of potential candidates and specific adverse effects. Uncertainty denotes the inability to provide accurate and precise quantitative assessments between a causing

Table 1 Overview of the management strategies

Management	Risk class	Extent of damage	Probability of occurrence	Strategies for action
Science-based	*Damocles* *Cyclops*	• High • High	• Low • Uncertain	• Reducing disaster potential • Ascertaining probability • Increasing resilience • Preventing surprises • Emergency management
Precautionary	*Pythia* *Pandora*	• Uncertain • Uncertain	• Uncertain • Uncertain	• Implementing precautionary principle • Developing substitutes • Improving knowledge • Reduction and containment • Emergency management
Discursive	*Cassandra* *Medusa*	• High • Low	• High • Low	• Consciousness-building • Confidence-building • Public participation • Risk communication • Contingency management

Source adapted from Klinke and Renn (2002)

agent and an effect. Finally, ambiguity denotes either the variability of (legitimate) interpretations based on identical observations or data assessments or the variability of normative implications for risk evaluation (judgment on tolerability or acceptability of a given risk).

In a case where scientific complexity is high and uncertainty and ambiguity are low, the challenge is to invite experts to deliberate with risk managers to understand complexity. Understanding the risks of oil platforms may be a good example of this. Although the technology is highly complex and many interacting devices lead to multiple accident scenarios, most possible pathways to a major accident can be modelled well in advance. The major challenge is to determine the limit to which one is willing to invest in resilience.

The second route concerns risk problems that are characterized by high uncertainty but low ambiguity. Expanded knowledge acquisition may help to reduce uncertainty. If, however, uncertainty cannot be reduced (or only reduced in the long run) by additional knowledge, a "precaution-based risk management" is required. Precaution-based risk management explores a variety of options: containment, diversification, monitoring, and substitution. The focal point here is to find an adequate and fair balance between over-cautiousness and insufficient caution. This argues for a reflective process involving stakeholders to ponder concerns, economic budgeting, and social evaluations.

For risk problems that are highly ambiguous (regardless of whether they are low or high on uncertainty and complexity), the third route recommends a "discourse-based management." Discourse management requires a participatory process involving stakeholders, especially the affected public. The aim of such a process is to produce a collective understanding among all stakeholders and the affected public about how to interpret the situation and how to design procedures for collectively justifying binding decisions on acceptability and tolerability that are considered legitimate. In such situations, the task of risk managers is to create a condition where those who believe that the risk is worth taking and those who believe otherwise are willing to respect diverse viewpoints and to construct and create strategies acceptable to the various stakeholders and interests.

In essence: The effectiveness and legitimacy of the risk governance process depends on the capability of management agencies to resolve complexity, characterize uncertainty and handle ambiguity by means of communication and deliberation.

4.2 *Instrumental Processing Involving Governmental Actors*

Dealing with linear risk issues, which are associated with low scores for complexity, scientific uncertainty and socio-political ambiguity, requires hardly any changes to conventional public policy-making. The data and information regarding such linear (routine) risk problems are provided by statistical analysis; law or statutory requirements determine the general and specific objectives; and the role of public policy is to ensure that all necessary safety and control measures are implemented and enforced (Klinke and Renn 2014). Traditional cost-benefit analyses including effectiveness and efficiency criteria are the instruments of political choice for finding the right balance between under- and over-regulation of risk-related activities and goods. In addition, monitoring the area is important to help prevent unexpected consequences. For this reason, linear risk issues can well be handled by departmental and agency staff and enforcement personnel of state-run governance institutions. The aim is to find the most cost-effective method for a desired regulation level. If necessary, stakeholders may be included in the deliberations as they have information and know-how that may help to make the measures more efficient. These risks are generally not systemic and are routine challenges for risk management agencies.

4.3 Epistemic Processing Involving Experts

Resolving complex risk problems requires dialogue and deliberation among experts. The main goal is to scan and review existing knowledge about the causal connections between an agent and potential consequences, to characterize the uncertainty of this relationship and to explore the evidence that supports these inferences. Involving members of various epistemic communities which demonstrate expertise and competence is the most promising step for producing more reliable and valid judgments about the complex nature of a given risk. Epistemic discourse is the instrument for discussing the conclusiveness and validity of cause-effect chains relying on available probative facts, uncertain knowledge and experience that can be tested for empirical traceability and consistency. The objective of such a deliberation is to find the most cogent description and explanation of the phenomenological complexity in question as well as a clarification of dissenting views (for example, by addressing the question which environmental and socio-economic impacts are to be expected in which areas and in what time frame). The deliberation among experts might generate a profile of the complexity of the given risk issue on selected inter-subjectively chosen criteria. The deliberation may also reveal that there is more uncertainty and ambiguity hidden in the case than the initial appraisers had anticipated (Birkmann 2011). It is advisable to include natural as well as social scientists in the epistemic discourse so that potential problems with risk perception and risk frames can be anticipated. Controversies would then be less of a surprise than is currently the case. Such epistemic discourse is meant to lead to adaptive management procedures that monitor the state of knowledge and proficiency in the field and adjust management responses according to the various levels of knowledge available at each time period. Epistemological discourses are well suited for risks that fall in the category of Damocles and Cyclops. They tend to be conventional risks but with a strong component of knowledge uncertainty.

4.4 Reflective Processing Involving Stakeholders

Characterizing and evaluating risks as well as developing and selecting appropriate management options for risk reduction and control in situations of high uncertainty poses particular challenges. How can risk managers characterize and evaluate the severity of a risk problem when the potential damage and its probability are unknown or highly uncertain? Scientific input is, therefore, only the first step in a series of steps constituting a more sophisticated evaluation process. It is crucial to compile the relevant data and information about the different types of uncertainties to inform the process of risk characterization. The outcome of the risk characterization process provides the foundation for a broader deliberative arena, in which not only policy makers and scientists, but also directly affected stakeholders and public interest groups ought to be involved in order to discuss and ponder the "right" balances and trade-offs between over- and under-protection (Renn and Schweizer 2009). This reflective involvement of stakeholders and interest groups pursues the purpose of finding a consensus on the extra margin of safety that potential victims would be willing to tolerate and potential beneficiaries of the risk would be willing to invest in to avoid potentially critical and catastrophic consequences. If too much precaution is applied, innovations may be impeded or even eliminated; if too little precaution is applied, society may experience the occurrence of undesired consequences. The crucial question here is how much uncertainty and ignorance the main stakeholders and public interest groups are willing to accept or tolerate in exchange for some potential benefit. Reflective discourses are best suited to deal with risks that fall in the category of Pythia and Pandora. They tend to be systemic but lack the high degree of ambiguity that characterize many systemic risks.

This issue has direct implications for another target in risk management: improving resilience. The concept of resilience has been used in many disciplines for different notions of being able to respond adequately when the system is under stress. It has been widely applied in ecological research and denotes the resistance of natural ecosystems to cope with stressors (Holling 1973). Resilience is focused on the ability and capacity of systems to resist shocks and to have the capability to deal and recover from threatening events (Rose 2007). This idea of resistance and recovery can also be applied to social systems (Norris et al. 2008). The main emphasis here is on organizational learning and institutional preparedness to cope with stress and disaster. Pulling from an interdisciplinary body of theoretical and policy-oriented literature, Longstaff et al. regard resilience as a function of resource robustness and adaptive capacity (Longstaff et al. 2010).

The governance framework suggested by the International Risk Governance Council (IRGC 2005) depicts resilience as a normative goal for risk management systems to deal with highly uncertain events or processes (surprises). It is seen as a property of risk-absorbing systems to withstand stress (objective resilience) but also the confidence of risk management actors to be able to master crisis situations (subjective resilience).

As the IRGC concept of resilience reflects the confidence of all actors to deal with even uncertain outcomes, it provides a mental guideline for the negotiations between beneficiaries and potential victims of risks that are typical for reflective discourses. Furthermore, this type of discourse explicitly addresses coping capacity and compensation schemes if the worst were to happen. The boundary between subjective and objective resilience is, however, fuzzy under the condition of effect uncertainty (Brown and Kulig 1996). In cases of known risks, past experience can demonstrate whether the degree of self-confidence was accurate and justified. Over long timespans one would expect an emerging congruence between objective and subjective resilience (learning by trial and error). However, for extremely rare events or highly uncertain outcomes, one necessarily relies on models of anticipation and expectations that will widely vary among different stakeholder groups, in particular those who benefit and those who will bear the risks. Furthermore, there will be lots of debates about the potential distribution of effects over time and space. The degree of coping capacity that is regarded as sufficient or justified for approving a new risk agent or a disaster management plan to become enacted depends therefore on a discourse between the directly affected groups of the population. Such a reflective involvement of policy makers, scientists, stakeholders and public interest groups can be accomplished through a spectrum of different procedures such as negotiated rule-making, mediation, round-table or open forums, advisory committees, and others (Rowe and Frewer 2000).

4.5 Participative Processing Involving the Wider Public

If risk problems are associated with high ambiguity, it is not enough to demonstrate that risk regulation addresses the public concerns of those directly affected by the impacts of the risk source. In these cases, the process of evaluation and management needs to be open to public input and new forms of deliberation. This corresponds with the participative aspect of resilience (Lorenz 2013). Such discursive activities should start with revisiting the question of proper framing. Is the issue really a risk problem or is it an issue of lifestyle or future vision? Often the benefits are contested as well as the risks. The debate about "designer babies" may illustrate the point that observers may be concerned not only about the social risks of intervening in the genetic code of humans but also about the acceptability of the desired goal to improve the performance of individuals (Hudson 2006). Thus, the controversy is often much broader than dealing with the direct risks only. The aim here is to find an overlapping consensus on the dimensions of ambiguity that need to be addressed in comparing risks and benefits, and balancing pros and cons. High ambiguity would require the most inclusive strategy for involvement because not only directly affected groups but also those indirectly affected should have an opportunity to contribute to this debate.

Resolving ambiguities in risk debates necessitates the participatory involvement of the public to openly discuss competing arguments, beliefs and values. Participatory involvement offers opportunities to resolve conflicting expectations through a process of identifying overarching common values, and to define options that will allow a desirable lifestyle without compromising the vision of others. Critical to success here is the establishment of equitable and just distribution rules when it comes to common resources and a common understanding of the scope, size and range of the problem, as well as the options for dealing with the problem (Wachinger et al. 2014). Unless there is some agreement on the boundaries of what is included, there is hardly any chance for a common solution. Such a common agreement will touch upon the coping capacity of systems to deal with different frames of risks, and not only with the physical impacts of risks. There are various social constructions of resilience that the participants associate with the management options. The set of possible procedures for involving the public includes citizen panels or juries, citizen forums, consensus conferences, public advisory committees and similar approaches (Hagendijk and Irwin 2006).

An overview of the different participation and stakeholder involvement requirements with respect to linear, complex, uncertain and ambiguous risks is displayed

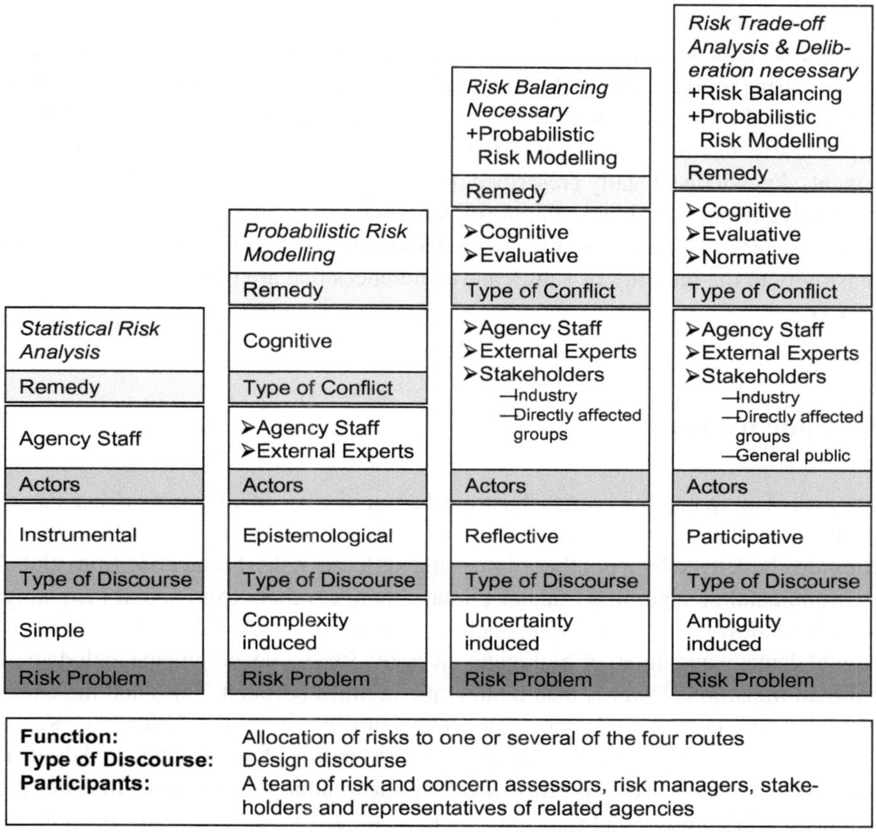

Fig. 2 The risk escalator: a guide to inclusive risk governance. *Source* adapted from Renn (2008, p. 280)

in Fig. 2 (Renn 2008). As is the case with all classifications, this scheme shows a simplified picture of the involvement process and it has been criticized for being too rigid in its linking of risk characteristics (complexity, uncertainty, and ambiguity) and specific forms of discourse and dialogue (Löftstedt and van Asselt 2008).

The central questions for policy makers are about the suitable approaches and instruments as well as the adequate risk assessment practices to understand the impacts of systemic risks and to assess and evaluate their contribution to health-related, environmental, financial and political risks (and, of course, opportunities). In addition, the link to strategic policy concerns as they relate to economic development and governance needs to be clarified. One of the most challenging topics here is the interpenetration of physical, environmental, economic and social manifestations of risks. Risk management is not only a task for risk management agencies, but also an imperative mandate for organizations dealing with the economic, financial, social and political ramifications.

It is not sufficient any more to look into the probability distribution of potential losses associated with a risk source. To establish a framework for good governance, a more stringent, logically well-structured and promising decision-making process is required. Risk managers need new principles and strategies, which are globally applicable to manage systemic risks. Good governance seems to rest on the three components: knowledge, legally prescribed procedures and social values. It has to reflect knowledge about functional relationships between triggers and effects, procedures of how to perform valid assessments and democratically legitimized evaluations and sensitivity to the plurality of values and preferences that are typical for a pluralistic society.

5 Conclusions

The goal of this paper has been to illustrate the significance of innovative risk management approaches to improve resilience and systemic risk governance. Current societies are challenged by a number of pressing systemic risks. Some arise from global environmental change, in particular climate change, others from social inequality, from breakdown of infrastructures including financial systems, from local environmental damage and threat of biological diversity. Recent developments include new political transitions towards post-democratic regimes (Crouch 2004) and the emergence of post-factual tendencies that underestimate the value of plurality (Keyes 2004). Until this day, we lack an adequate understanding of the structure and dynamics of systemic risks. The stochastic and non-linear nature of these risks impedes the application of conventional risk assessment methods based on the probability function of adverse effects. The focus should rather be on a better analysis of the systemic properties of risks and their adequate management strategies.

For this purpose, this chapter addressed the three major risk characteristics—complexity, uncertainty and ambiguity. These three aspects were used to develop risk categories, named after Greek mythological figures, which illustrate different types and manifestations of systemic risks. This classification resulted in four major risk management and discourse strategies: beginning with simple risk management in which none of these characteristics and capacity requirements were involved, and culminating with discourse-based management in which all three characteristics, complexity, uncertainty and ambiguity were combined.

Whereas the analysis of simple and (to some degree) complex problems is better served by relying on the physical understanding of experienced resilience, uncertain and ambiguous problems demand the integration of social constructions and mental models of resilience, operationalized as confidence in one's coping capacity, for both understanding and managing these problems (Bloesch et al. 2015). The distinction of risks according to risk characteristics and types not only highlights deficits in our knowledge concerning a risk issue, but also points the way forward for the selection of the appropriate management options. Thus, the risk governance framework attributes an important function to public and stakeholder participation, as well as risk communication, in the risk governance process. The classification suggests efficient and adequate public or stakeholder participation procedures. The concerns of stakeholders and/or the public are integrated in the risk appraisal phase via concern assessment. Furthermore, stakeholder and public participation are an established part of risk management. The optimum participation method depends on the characteristics of the risk issue. The need for finding an agreement on what constitutes an adaptive, coping and participative response to ensuring resilience underlines the necessity to understand and comprehend the objective and subjective nature of resilience.

References

Birkmann J (2011) First-and second-order adaptation to natural hazards and extreme events in the context of climate change. Nat Hazards 58(2):811–840

Bloesch J, von Hauff M, Mainzer K, Mohan V, Renn O, Risse V, Song Y, Takeuchi K, Wilderer P (2015) Sustainable development integrated in the concept of resilience. Probl Sustain Dev 10(1):7–14

Brown D, Kulig J (1996) The concept of resiliency: theoretical lessons from community research. Health Can Soc 4:29–52

Crouch C (2004) Post democracy. Polity, Cambridge

Hagendijk R, Irwin A (2006) Public deliberation and governance: engaging with science and technology in contemporary Europe. Minerva 44(2):167–184

Helbing D (2010) Systemic risks in society and economics. International Risk Governance Council. https://www.irgc.org/IMG/pdf/Systemic_Risks_Helbing2.pdf

Helbing D (2012) New ways to promote sustainability and social well-being in a complex, strongly interdependent world: the FuturICT approach. Why society is a complex matter. Springer, Berlin, pp 55–60

Holling CS (1973) Resilience and stability of ecological systems. Annu Rev Ecol Syst 4(1):1–23

Hudson KL (2006) Preimplantation genetic diagnosis: public policy and public attitudes. Fertil Steril 85(6):1638–1645

IRGC (International Risk Governance Council) (2005) Risk governance: towards an integrative approach. White paper no. 1, ITGC, Geneva

Kasperson JX, Kasperson RE, Pidgeon N, Slovic P (2003) The social amplification of risk: assessing fifteen years of research and theory. In: Pidgeon N, Kasperson RE, Slovic P (eds) The social amplification of risk. Cambridge University Press, Cambridge, pp 13–46

Kaufman GG, Scott KE (2003) What is systemic risk, and do bank regulators retard or contribute to it? Indep Rev 7(3):371–391

Keyes R (2004) The post-truth era. St. Martin's Press, New York

Klinke A, Renn O (1999) Prometheus unbound. Challenges of risk evaluation, risk classification, and risk management. Akademie für Technikfolgenabschätzung in Baden-Württemberg. Working paper no. 153

Klinke A, Renn O (2002) A new approach to risk evaluation and management: risk-based, precaution-based, and discourse-based strategies. Risk Anal Int J 22(6):1071–1094

Klinke A, Renn O (2012) Adaptive and integrative governance on risk and uncertainty. J Risk Res 15(3):273–292

Klinke A, Renn O (2014) Expertise and experience: a deliberative system of a functional division of labor for post-normal risk governance. Innov Eur J Soc Sci Res 27(4):442–465

Löftstedt R, van Asselt M (2008) A framework for risk governance revisited. In: Renn O, Walker K (eds) Global risk governance. Concept and practice using the IRGC framework. Springer, Dordrecht, pp 77–86
Longstaff PH, Armstrong NJ, Perrin K, Parker WM, Hidek MA (2010) Building resilient communities: a preliminary framework for assessment. Homel Secur Aff VI(3):1–23
Lorenz DF (2013) The diversity of resilience: contributions from a social science perspective. Nat Hazards 67(1):7–24
Norris FH, Stevens SP, Pfefferbaum B, Wyche KF, Pfefferbaum RL (2008) Community resilience as a metaphor, theory, set of capacities, and strategy for disaster readiness. Am J Commun Psychol 41(1–2):127–150
Nursimulu A (2015) Governance of slow-developing catastrophic risks: fostering complex adaptive system and resilience thinking. SSRN. https://d6.doi.org/10.2139/ssrn.2830581
OECD (2003) Emerging risks in the 21st century. An agenda for action. OECD, Paris. https://www.oecd.org/futures/globalprospects/37944611.pdf
Renn O (2008) Risk governance. Coping with uncertainty in a complex world. Earthscan, London
Renn O (2011) The social amplification/attenuation of risk framework: application to climate change. Wiley Interdiscip Rev Clim Change 2(2):154–169
Renn O (2014) Das Risikoparadox. Warum, wir uns vor dem Falschen fürchten. Fisher, Frankfurt/Main
Renn O (2015) Are we afraid of the wrong things? Statistics, psychology and the risk paradox. In: Union Investment (ed) The measurement of risk. Union Investment International, Frankfurt am Main, pp. 24–35
Renn O (2016) Systemic risks: the new kid on the block. Environ Sci Policy Sustain Dev 58(2):26–36
Renn O, Klinke A (2016) Complexity, uncertainty and ambiguity in inclusive risk governance. In: Andersen TJ (ed) The Routledge companion to strategic risk management. Routledge, New York, pp 13–30
Renn O, Schweizer PJ (2009) Inclusive risk governance: concepts and application to environmental policy making. Environ Policy Gov 19(3):174–185
Renn O, Lucas K, Haas A, Jaeger C (2017) Things are different today: the challenge of global systemic risks. J Risk Res 1–15
Rosa E, McCright A, Renn O (2013) The risk society revisited: social theory and risk governance. Temple University Press, Philadelphia
Rose A (2007) Economic resilience to natural and man-made disasters: multidisciplinary origins and contextual dimensions. Environ Hazards 7(4):383–398
Rowe G, Frewer LJ (2000) Public participation methods: a framework for evaluation. Sci Technol Human Values 25(1):3–29
van Asselt M (2000) Perspectives on uncertainty and risk. Springer, Netherlands, Dordrecht and Boston
Wachinger G, Renn O, Wist SK, Steinhilber SM, Triemer U (2014) Using participation to create resilience: how to involve citizens in designing a hospital system? Environ Syst Decis 34(2):208–223
WBGU, German Advisory Council on Global Change (2000) World in transition. Strategies for managing global environmental risks. Annual report 1998. Springer, Berlin
Wiedemann PM, Mertens J, Schütz H (2000) Risikoabschätzung und Erarbeitung von Optionen für mögliche Vorsorgekonzepte für nichtionisierende Strahlung. Arbeiten zur Risiko-Kommunikation, Heft 81. Forschungszentrum KFA, Jülich
Wynne B, Dressel K (2001) Cultures of uncertainty—transboundary risks and BSE in Europe. In: Linnerooth-Bayer J, Löfstedt RE, Sjöstedt G (eds) Transboundary risk management. Earthscan, London, pp 121–154

MIX
Papier aus verantwortungsvollen Quellen
Paper from responsible sources
FSC® C105338

If you have any concerns about our products,
you can contact us on
ProductSafety@springernature.com

In case Publisher is established outside the EU,
the EU authorized representative is:
Springer Nature Customer Service Center GmbH
Europaplatz 3, 69115 Heidelberg, Germany

Printed by Libri Plureos GmbH
in Hamburg, Germany